KNOCKIN'
DOORZ
DOWN

KNOCKIN' DOORZ DOWN

A Story of Breaking Through the Darkness
and Finding Redemption

CARLOS EDUARDO VIEIRA

Livingston, California

Published by KDD Media Company, Livingston, California

Hardcover ISBN: 978-1-7345487-0-9
Paperback ISBN: 978-1-7345487-1-6
e-book ISBN: 978-1-7345487-2-3

Library of Congress Control Number: 2020901866

Book design by Graphique Designs, LLC

Jacket images provided by iStock.com and Shutterstock.com:
© SDI Productions/iStock.com, © Hikesterson/iStock.com,
© Nosyrevy/Shutterstock.com, © Conrado/Shutterstock.com,
© Netfalls Remy Musser/Shutterstock.com, © Krivosheev Vitaly/
Shutterstock.com, © Ksw Photographer/Shutterstock.com

Printed in the United States of America

10 9 8 7 6 5 4 3 2 1

To my wife, Aysia.
Thank you for always believing in me
and for supporting me in writing this book.
I love you!

CONTENTS

AUTHOR'S NOTE

This is a work of nonfiction. I have tried to re-create events, locales, and conversations from my memories of them. In some instances, I have changed the names of individuals and places in order to maintain their anonymity. I have also changed some identifying characteristics and details, such as physical properties, occupations, and places of residence. Some events have been compressed or conflated, and some dialogue has been re-created.

A QUESTION OF DOORS

During the early years of my life, I often felt as if I was locked in a room that had multiple doors, each representing a choice I could make.

I rarely chose the right one. In fact, it took years before I finally knocked down the door that changed my life forever.

Prior to that, as a young adult, I was on a quest to discover myself. I tried many different doors—some leading to years of chaos, others to dead ends, and still others to loving relationships—but those, too, died.

Many of my decisions were influenced by friends, family, and professionals who thought they knew what was best for me. But I eventually learned that what *others* thought I *should* do was not necessarily the *right* thing to do, at least for me, and it certainly wasn't sufficient to create lifelong change.

After years of revolving doors and bad choices, I finally had an epiphany, and that's where this book begins.

As you'll read, the events that happened one momentous night changed everything and became the catalyst for total transformation.

It was only in that moment that I fully understood what I needed to do next. That was the door that ultimately led to my salvation, to healing myself and finding a sense of peace and happiness, allowing me to become the person I was always meant to be.

This is the story of the son of an immigrant who was raised on a sweet potato farm in Central California. I was an honest, reliable, well-intentioned boy who worked hard, played hard, and fell in love three times, producing two wonderful children. But along the way, darkness enveloped me, and I fell into habits that almost destroyed me.

Miraculously, I survived and even thrived, thanks to the redemption offered by a sport and a way of life that were new to me. Now I feel as if I'm finally walking through the *right* doors, contributing to the world and helping others make the best choices for themselves.

As you read on, I hope you will be inspired to tap into your own true passions. I hope you will find healthful activities and loving relationships that make life all it can be. I also hope what I've written will help you if you're struggling with anything—an addiction, a tough relationship, a money problem, a health challenge. I know how you feel. I've been to those dark places. But this book is meant to open a new door and turn on the light.

CHAPTER 1

THE LONGER YOU HOLD IT, THE HIGHER YOU GET

I sat at the bottom of the stairs in shadowy light. Behind me, the dark interior stairway led to the second floor of a house, but it was not my house. In fact, I had never been there before, and the house did not belong to anyone I knew.

So why was I there? And how did I get there?

As I sat, breathing heavily, dazed, I rubbed my hands together, not knowing what else to do with them. I was jittery and couldn't hold still because of the large amount of cocaine I'd done that night, which was coursing through my nervous system.

Even though it was a cool evening, sweat rolled down my forehead. Was it from kicking in my neighbor's door? Partly, yes. But it was also caused by panic, a state of mind that left me irrational, doing things that made no sense to anyone, not even me.

There I was in the middle of the night, slumped on the doorstep of someone else's house, breaking and entering, invading their space while not understanding why I had done it.

I asked myself, *What's happening? How did my life get to this point? And now that I've hit bottom, what comes next?*

To understand this night—which I have come to call *The Night*—we need to travel back in time, to the beginning of my life as a cocaine addict.

I drew in the smoke and held it, trying to get the most from the sweet-smelling joint in my hand. I then exhaled out the open window of my truck, which I had parked alongside an almond orchard on the outskirts of Livingston, California.

It was a typically hot summer night in the Central Valley, but there was a slight breeze. I could see the leaves of the almond trees fluttering as I stared beyond the farmlands toward the dusty horizon.

My friend Doug, whom I had known most of my life, sat in the passenger seat next to me. I always envied him because he was one of the most popular and athletic guys in school, plus he had a nice car. He also had lots of girls running after him.

That night in the truck, Doug held two Ziploc bags in his lap: the smaller one contained powder cocaine, and the larger one was filled with baking soda.

Doug grinned at me. "Pretty cool, huh?"

I nodded, finished my joint, and watched with fascination as he started the process of turning the cocaine powder into something he could smoke.

At that point, I had no interest in smoking cocaine. I was a twenty-year-old who had just left college and had plans to learn the family business—farming—so I could eventually take over and run it. But on that night of escape, all I cared about was smoking my joint. Yet I never thought of myself as an addict. That's for sure. Shoot, I never smoked weed until college. Back then, in the early 1990s, I partied, drank a little, and smoked weed, but I thought of cocaine as too hard-core for me. I would never try it.

However, I was utterly fascinated with Doug's ritual process.

"You gotta get the right mix," he said, bending over as he prepared the powder. "The better blend you have, the better rock you get."

First he bent the spoon so it would sit level on the center console. He mixed the cocaine with the baking soda, then added a tiny bit of water to the spoon, careful not to spill any.

"Here—hold this lighter, just like this," he told me.

I followed his instructions. As the flame heated the bottom of the spoon, the mixture started to bubble. Doug unbent a paper clip and used it to stir the mixture in the spoon, moving it back and forth until the powder-and-water mix turned into something like a gel. Then he replaced the paper clip with a knife, which he used to scrape the mixture out of the spoon and onto his hand. As it hardened, it transformed into a small rock, like a tiny marble. Doug always cooked small amounts, around half a gram at a time.

Several months later, I learned that the baking soda removed the impurities from the cocaine, made it stronger, and turned it into something you could smoke. That night in the truck, however, I was still quite naive about the process. But Doug was a good teacher.

Once he had a good rock, he pulled out a Chore Boy copper scrubber and tore off a piece of it.

"Hold the lighter again," he said.

He held the fragment over the flame, removing the copper coating, and wiped the burned residue from the wire with his fingers after it cooled, leaving his fingers black. He then pulled a six-inch piece of automotive brake line out of his pocket, which he used as a makeshift pipe, and shoved the cleaned strip of scouring pad into the end of it. This would act as a screen to hold the rock.

He placed the rock on top of the screen and heated it, then he ceremoniously raised the pipe in the air while he continued to light it. Then he would bring the pipe down while puffing in the smoke. He would continue to light the scouring pad while inhaling, holding the smoke in his lungs as long as he possibly could.

"The longer you hold it, the higher you get," he told me. "Your ears start to ring. You experience instant euphoria throughout your whole body. It feels great, man. You sure you don't want some?"

"No, thanks," I told him. "I'm good."

I admit I was curious, but not curious enough to try it.

He snorted a laugh.

"Why do you do it?" I asked him.

"It's the greatest high you'll ever have," he answered with confidence. "Hits you like a freight train. Tastes sweet, like candy. You'd love it. I know you would."

"I'm good," I said again, looking out at the stars and wondering if he was right. Maybe I *would* love it.

He took another hit off his homemade pipe and threw his head back against the headrest. "That is some good shit."

Watching Doug and his smoking ritual was a little scary.

"You ever think about getting clean?" I asked him.

"Sure, sure, I think about it. It's hard."

"I know that," I told him. "But you're hurting your family. Missing out on time with your kids and seeing them grow up."

"Carlos, I know that. But I just love it. I need it."

"Is it worth it, though?"

Doug looked out the window and didn't reply.

I didn't want to preach at him, but it didn't feel right to me—a guy spending all his time and money on drugs while he had a family at home who needed him and people at work who depended on him.

We hung out a lot together like this, parked in my truck in the orchards or on one of the dirt roads that ran along the banks of the irrigation canals that kept the sweet potato fields watered. I would smoke weed, and Doug would prepare and smoke his cocaine.

I repeatedly tried to convince him that he needed help, but he didn't listen to me. Why would he? I was four years younger than he was, and I had no idea what to say or how to help. But I figured he was safe as long as he was with me, so that was something, I guess.

"You still missing work?" I asked him. There I was, preaching again.

Doug had an important job, and he had an opportunity to move up the ladder in the company he was working for. But half the time, he didn't show up.

"Sometimes I make it in. Don't worry, man. I have this handled. They're not gonna fire me. They need me."

Your wife and kids need you, too, I thought. I guess for a twenty-year-old I was pretty adult, feeling more responsible for him than he was for himself.

He measured out some more cocaine and baking soda into the spoon and started the process again. We talked, and he smoked until there was no cocaine left.

"C'mon, Doug, you're out," I said. "It's time to go home."

He looked at the bag, the pipe, and the spoon. They were all empty.

"Damn. How did I run out?" he asked, disoriented and confused.

"You smoked it all. Come on. Time to go."

"Let's go get more."

"No."

Sometimes he would listen to me and go home without a fight. But other times it was a battle to convince him that the night should be over.

Time after time, Doug and I hit the same routine. Sometimes it was once or twice a week, sometimes more often. I would drive, and we would find a spot on the banks of an irrigation canal or in an orchard, where Doug would make rocks of cocaine while I smoked weed.

I would often help him prepare his rock, mostly holding lighters and acting as his lab assistant. He enjoyed describing the process while he was doing it, as if I hadn't already heard it dozens of times.

He always offered me a hit, of course, and I always said no.

Until the day I said yes.

I don't remember that moment with any kind of clarity. I don't know exactly where the truck was parked or what prompted me to finally cave in. But that time, when he asked if I wanted a hit, I said, "Sure. I'll give it a try."

Up until that point, I'd always declined—not because I was afraid of getting hooked but because I felt I was *above* that kind of drug use. I'd only started smoking weed a couple of years earlier, in college, and based on my limited experience, I saw myself as a "higher-caliber" drug user who could maintain my composure and my cool at all times. In fact, I prided myself in being master of my destiny, always in control of any situation. In high school, I was a jock, not a straight-A student, but I kept my grades up because I wanted to play sports. In the classroom, I was a joker and a clown, though I could be serious when it came to focusing on what needed to be done. In short, I was a clean-cut kid from a good home, and I never, ever thought drugs would become a problem for me. So when I took that first hit, I told myself that one little hit wouldn't hurt me.

But I have to say that Doug was right. The euphoria was instant. I felt high immediately . . . like, in two seconds. The feeling was amazing. My mind and body felt as if they had gotten an immediate jump start. I suddenly had incredible energy, which surged through me, making me feel like I was on top of the world. Every hair on my body was standing on end. I felt like everything was speeding up. As Doug had said, there was a lingering sweetness to the aftertaste. I had never felt better in my entire life.

"Amazing, huh?" Doug prompted, proud of himself.

"Yeah," I said, relishing the ecstatic feeling of electricity passing through every nerve in my body.

We sat there, savoring it. It was 2:00 a.m. by the time I started up the truck and drove home.

THE LONGER YOU HOLD IT, THE HIGHER YOU GET

The next morning, I told myself, *Yeah, the high was great, but I don't want to do it again.* Weed was socially acceptable, like drinking beer. But cocaine? That went too far, and I wasn't interested in going there. I would certainly never be addicted, as Doug was. What he was doing by getting me high was for *his* benefit, not mine. He needed someone to support him, to get high with, but I didn't want to be that person. I was better than that. I clung to that thought.

But over the next few months, Doug and I continued getting together, though he started to disappear from time to time, his behavior unpredictable. Eventually, I lost touch with him. I heard that he left the country, left his wife and kids, and was out searching for a new life somewhere else.

My days of smoking cocaine had ended along with that relationship. Or so I told myself.

CHAPTER 2

JUST ONE, AGAIN AND AGAIN

Around six months after Doug left, I met up with some buddies at a party hosted by my friend Mark. By that time, the evenings I used to spend with Doug had been replaced by parties like this one. The gatherings were almost always held on weekends, because during the week I stayed clean and sober, working at A. V. Thomas Produce, the sweet potato packing plant my father owned. Having left college because I had little interest in it, I was intent on moving up in the family business, though I was easily distracted by parties, girls, and drugs.

"Hey, Carlos, what's up?" Mark called as he came to greet me.

"Not much," I said. "Just ready to have a good time. Glad it's the weekend."

"Me too, bro. Come in; grab a drink."

Music thumped from the speakers in the living room. Beer and liquor bottles lined the tables and kitchen counter, and red plastic cups were scattered over every surface. I moved through the house, saying hello to various friends as I made my way to the bar, then settled in to hang out with a small group in the backyard. It was like any other party. We talked about work, life, and girls, just joked around—the usual party chatter. After a while, Mark came up and asked me to follow him to the garage.

"Sure," I said, and we headed out.

There were a couple of other guys there, sitting around a rickety wooden table.

"You want to try something new?" Mark asked.

"What do you have in mind?"

"You want to do a line of coke?"

I'm not sure why I said yes. I had vowed that I was never going to do it again. But I figured I had smoked it before, so snorting it couldn't hurt. I was already feeling buzzed from the alcohol, so my inhibitions were pretty loose at that point.

The guys around the table were already chopping up the coke, and I thought, *Do I really want to do this?* I paused for a second before deciding. *Screw it: How is it going to hurt? I'll do one line, just this one time.*

The first sensation was a burning one, then I felt the drug hit me in the back of the head. I brushed my nose and sniffed.

"Damn, bro. That burns! Is this really cocaine?"

Mark laughed.

"Seriously, that didn't feel right. Was that really cocaine?"

One of the other guys laughed, too, as if he was in on the joke. I felt like they were all playing me. I didn't know what that drug was, but it sure didn't feel like the same type of high I had when I smoked coke with Doug. Could snorting it be that different? I didn't like the feeling at all, and it pissed me off.

"Mark, don't lie to me. If that wasn't coke, just tell me what it was."

"That was crystal meth," Mark told me. "Do you like it?"

"No. It burns. And it hit the back of my head like a hammer."

"Not everybody likes it. I just wanted you to give it a shot."

"Well, don't lie to me to get me to try shit. Next time don't bullshit me. Just tell me the truth."

"Okay. Sorry, man," Mark said.

I was infuriated that he'd tricked me, and I was disappointed in myself for trying crystal meth, not to mention any hard drug. Crystal meth was considered a poor man's drug—super addictive and guaranteed to destroy your life. I didn't want to be associated with it. The last thing I wanted was to be known as a meth head. Meth addicts were considered the lowest step on the drug-culture ladder, totally strung out. The negative effects can include weird sleep patterns, hyperactivity, nausea, delusions of grandeur, and increased aggressiveness and irritability.

But it was too late to do anything about it now. The deed was done.

"Let's just get back to the party," I snarled, still pissed off.

The party lasted for hours into the night, and the high stayed with me the entire time. I have to say that experiencing meth helped me understand why people like it so much. The sensation is exhilarating, because it jump-starts your energy and keeps it up for hours after you do just one line, whereas cocaine might only keep you high for an hour or less. After that, you want more coke to keep it going. For the average drug user, that could get quite expensive and out of reach pretty fast. Some people I partied with were scared to try cocaine for that reason. If they got hooked, they couldn't afford to keep the high going.

Even though I didn't snort cocaine that night, I did a few weeks later while sitting around at another friend's house after work. I was getting bored with just the two of us hanging out, talking about nothing, and I wanted a diversion.

"Let's go over to Jared's and party there," I said.

He agreed. "Sure, man," he said.

Jared was an older guy, more mature than the rest of us, someone who smoked weed and was experienced in doing other drugs as well. Though he was never my drug connection, we would get high on weed sometimes.

We got to Jared's and walked around the house to his garage workshop, where he tinkered with electronics, cars—anything mechanical that held his attention. The moment we entered, he gestured to a line of powder on his workbench, bent down, and snorted it.

"You want to try?" he asked, offering us the rolled-up twenty-dollar bill he was using as a snorting straw.

After the incident at Mark's I wanted to be sure of what I was being offered, so I asked, "What is it?"

"Cocaine," he stated proudly. "Go ahead."

I looked over at my friend, then back at Jared. No one seemed to be smirking or putting me on, so I thought, *Why not? It's just one line.*

It was the line that would change my life.

I instantly felt euphoric. My senses sharpened. An incredible energy surged through me. Once again, I felt better than I ever had in my life. The taste and the feel of it in my throat and in my sinuses was thrilling. It was like candy for both my mind and my body.

Feeling high and invincible, Mark, Jared, and I decided to go out and look for some fun. We were headed toward the outskirts of Modesto, a flat, rural area populated by farmworkers, factory workers, and kids like us who were looking for some diversion from the boredom of our daily lives. That night, we hit all the hole-in-the-wall bars in town, continuing the party as long as we could. I felt amazing—alive and energized. With the coke coursing through my system, I felt powerful and invincible. What cocaine did for me was incredible, and I didn't want that feeling to ever end.

Just one hit. Just one line. Just one drink.

These are famous last words for many people who are or have been addicted to drugs or alcohol. It's the last thing they say before they spiral down the road of addiction, hitting bottom, vowing to stop, then relapsing, no matter how long they've been clean and sober.

I was always someone who couldn't imagine being addicted to *anything.* I never thought I would try hard drugs, let alone get hooked on them. The problem is, when you hang around long enough with people who do drugs, you'll eventually end up taking "just one hit," snorting "just one line," or having "just one taste." So yes, your friends will keep offering, and no matter how many times you refuse, you'll eventually give in. In short, who you hang out with is who you *become*.

You can try to be the one person who's different. You can go on thinking that what your friends are doing won't affect you or damage your life and health. You can even appoint yourself the designated driver to make sure you stay sober. But the odds are slim that you'll keep refusing and never try what they offer. It's far too much of a temptation.

That's what I wish I had known before I tried hard drugs. I wish I could have repeated it to myself until it sunk in.

I guarantee you won't become an addict the first time you try hard drugs. But once you open that door, you'll be more susceptible to letting it become a habit, and once you get into that habit, you'll get attached to the effect the drug has on your mind and body. You'll fall in love with the person you *think* you are when you're high, because that person seems to be more clever, more attractive, and more interesting than the person you are when you're clean and sober. You start to crave that feeling, and you seek it constantly. You look forward to the escape drugs provide from your routine, your humdrum reality. You also tell yourself that you can function— drive a car, go to school, go to work, and manage relationships.

It's all a bunch of crap.

The reason I'm telling my story is not to lecture you or to tell you how to live but to share my experience as a cautionary tale. Honestly, I never believed any drug could take over my life. But then again, I never dreamed there was a drug that could make me feel the way cocaine did.

CHAPTER 3

LIVINGSTON

Everything I've told you up until now has been about my days as a young man hanging out on the streets of the Central Valley, smoking weed, partying with friends, and moving on to harder drugs. No, I wasn't yet a hard-core addict, but I was sure on my way to becoming one.

Before I hit the age of twenty, it was inconceivable for me to imagine myself as a drug addict or a user of any kind. To understand what I'm talking about, and what a responsible kid I was as a student at Livingston High School, we have to go back to the very beginning.

My parents, Manuel and Laurinda Vieira, were both born in Portugal, my dad on the island of Pico, in the Azores, and my mom on the mainland, in the north. My mom's father, Francisco, had immigrated to Rio de Janeiro in 1952, leaving behind his wife, Maria, and his three kids—John, Laurinda, and Arlindo. (It was normal back then for the man of the house to take off looking for a better life for his family.) Four years later, in 1956, the entire family joined him in Rio.

Meanwhile, my dad, Manuel, didn't move to Brazil until he was seventeen, sent there to live on his own by his parents, Olympia and Eduardo, so he could avoid mandatory enlistment in the Portuguese army. Also left behind were Manuel's sister, Maria, and brother, Arthur.

As fate would have it, Manuel and Laurinda met when my

father was nineteen. They fell in love and married, then had three children in quick succession: my older brother, Ricardo; my sister, Marcia; and me, all of us born in Rio de Janeiro. Then, in 1972, when I was a baby, we moved to California.

Our winding up in the United States was a matter of fate. My parents originally came to California for a short trip—to attend my uncle Arthur's wedding, held in the tiny farming town of Gustine. But after just a few weeks of visiting, my dad realized he could provide a better life for his family in the United States, so he made the life-changing decision to stay. Arthur, his brother, grew many different types of produce, and he offered Dad a job working on the farm.

At the time, my mom, Ricardo, Marcia, and I went back to Rio de Janeiro while Dad worked until he could send for us. When we were ready to join him, my uncle served as a sponsor, which in those days would allow family members to immigrate.

For the first few years we lived in a little house in Gustine. My dad worked long, hard hours in the fields, driving a tractor all day in the hot sun and in other horrible weather.

Needless to say, we were poor. As a stay-at-home mom with three small kids to raise, my devoted mother took care of us and contributed in whatever way was necessary. She certainly did the best she could with the little we had. All of us wore hand-me-down clothes, but because my mom was a good seamstress, she kept them all in good repair. Sure, I wore secondhand shoes, too, but no matter our material circumstances, I was thankful for everything we had. More than anything else, we were a secure, loving family, so the material things were much less important.

When I was five years old, good fortune hit. Another relative— my paternal grandfather's brother, Antonio Vieira Tomas—offered to sell my dad his small sweet potato packing facility and twenty acres of farmland. Antonio had first immigrated to the United States from Portugal in 1920, settling in Newman, California.

This part of California, as he discovered, was one of the most fertile places in the country, with the warm climate and sandy soil necessary to grow sweet potatoes. So in 1960, he founded A. V. Thomas Produce, a small packing shed in downtown Livingston. That's how it all started.

Uncle Antonio was very impressed with my father's willingness to work and his passion for business. My father had earned a degree in business administration before coming to the United States and had learned hands-on farming by working for my uncle Arthur. Now it was time for Uncle Antonio to sell the sweet potato part of his business to my father.

It turned out to be the deal of a lifetime for my family. Dad became the proud new owner of A. V. Thomas Produce, which gave him a much greater sense of security and independence. However, it meant that the whole family would have to work. Whenever we weren't in school, my siblings and I would pack sweet potatoes, assemble boxes, and sweep the floors while my mom helped with everything from bookkeeping to packing. Dad did everything, too, including driving a forklift and handling sales. I was only five years old when I started.

There was so much to do that I was occupied all the time and never bored, unlike many of the kids I went to school with. Even if I was sick with a cold and couldn't go to school, I still ended up at the packinghouse because my mom had to take me with her while she worked. I was there in sickness and in health, which turned out to be a sign of things to come.

I quickly discovered that I needed to work hard for what I wanted, and I learned the importance of saving money. As a kid who loved fast cars, I dreamed of buying my own car someday, so I opened a savings account and put money into it as soon I started earning wages at the plant. I wanted to be ready.

I can honestly say that my parents raised us very well. They taught us right from wrong and never physically or emotionally abused us. Sometimes people who become addicted to drugs and alcohol tell horror stories about family dysfunction and various forms of abuse. But that was not the case with me. Our home was a happy place, filled with laughter, family gatherings, and great Portuguese food, including Mom's favorites—marinated pork, kale soup, salted codfish, rice pudding, and, of course, sweet potatoes. Neither of my parents used drugs or abused alcohol, and they both instilled in all three of us the idea that we could be whatever we wanted to be as long as we worked hard and earned what we got. If we didn't do more or become more, that was on us. Our lives were ours to live. It was an incredibly wise and loving way to raise kids—with a great work ethic and an emphasis on independence.

But it wasn't just hard work all the time. My dad believed in the value of team sports and encouraged me to try a variety of athletic activities. Between football in the fall, track and field in the spring, and basketball in the winter, I played sports year-round, and I excelled at it. I was an athletic guy, six feet tall, two hundred pounds, and in great shape mentally and physically. When I wasn't playing sports, I was working for the family business. I was seldom idle.

During these teenage years, I was almost totally focused on school, sports, and work—so unlike a lot of other kids my age, I didn't like to party. In fact, I had so much to do that I rarely drank or went to parties, and I never tried drugs in high school. That lifestyle seemed pointless to me.

Because I had been kept super busy from such a young age, I had developed a need to be occupied and involved in activities and projects all the time. I also loved taking on the role of a leader, something I did by starting clubs and organizing events in high school. My entrepreneurial spirit was already developing, so I got deeply involved in student government and other school functions. I was the captain of various sports teams—and frequently the MVP (most valuable player)—the head of several committees, and the primary organizer of a number of extracurricular activities.

Even with all that keeping me busy, I joined the school band and a Portuguese musical group that my dad started. I began by playing drums but moved on to trumpet, which I played all through my school years.

As soon as I turned sixteen and got my driver's license, I bought a car using the $8,500 I'd saved through my working years. But it wasn't just *any* car . . . it was a 1971 Porsche 911! This was my dream machine, a two-door high-performance rear-engine sports car, an incredible trophy for a teenage kid.

But because it was old and orange, I had to improve not only how it looked but also how it ran. Of course I had to install a fancy stereo system so I could blast music while cruising the streets of Merced and Modesto. The car became a central part of my life. I would work all week to get my car ready for those Friday and Saturday nights of cruising, feeling incredibly grown-up and independent.

In short, I was busy and engaged all the time. I felt happy, fulfilled, and accomplished. But like many kids my age, after high school graduation I found myself needing to decide what was next. I could either stay in the area and work at the sweet potato company or I could go to college to play football. But I initially rejected both those options because I felt as if I wanted a different, less conventional career path, something besides what I already knew.

In the end, I decided to go to school in Southern California, so I enrolled at Golden West College, in Huntington Beach. My parents supported me in that effort, and Dad wanted me to study business, though at that point, I didn't have a particular major in mind. I took some general-ed classes and figured I would decide where to go from there. My family paid for my tuition and rent, but I had to earn the rest. I got a part-time job at a shoe store. When you put the whole picture together, I was very excited about getting away from farm life and living on my own.

But there was one person I was really going to miss at college: my high school girlfriend, Sandra. We started dating when I was fifteen, after I'd been chasing a lot of different girls. But when I met Sandra, that was it—she was the one for me. She was a beautiful Mariah Carey look-alike and a straight-A student. She was on the shy side and innocent, raised in a very stable family with all the right values, just like mine. I loved her, and we spent as much time together as we could. When it was time for me to go away to college, we tried the long-distance-relationship thing, but that didn't last. At first, I missed her so much that on Friday nights after I was finished with work and classes, I'd drive five hours to Winton to spend the weekends with her.

She lived with her mother and stepfather, and even though they adored me, I had to sneak into her bedroom through the window to spend the night with her. On Sunday nights, I'd race back down to Southern California. But after a while, we both felt that we needed a break to experience other things during the times when we were forced to be away from each other.

Yes, college life got more "interesting" after Sandra and I broke up. That was when my rebellious side came out. As an eighteen-year-old, I had a car, I lived on my own, and I was a free man. I started drinking more, smoking weed and cigarettes, and having parties in my apartment. I had always had a lot of fun in life, for sure, but without parental supervision, I had time to experiment and experience new things. Even though I'd been offered a football scholarship and other opportunities for school involvement, I was tired of sports. The whole school thing had lost its appeal, too. In fact, I eventually stopped going to classes and spent my time just hanging out, not doing much of anything.

Then one day my father called me.

"Hey, Dad, what's up?"

"Carlos, I'm tired of working. I want to retire, and I want to do it soon."

"That's great, Dad."

"Your brother doesn't want to run the company, so I have a couple of choices. Either you can come back and learn to run it, or I can sell it."

"Sell it? Dad, no—don't do that."

"It's okay if this isn't what you want to do, Carlos. You're welcome to do something else. But if I'm going to retire soon, I need to make a decision quickly."

"Let me think about it and call you back," I told him.

My brother, Ricardo (we all call him Rick), four years older than I am, had his own personal issues going on, so he wasn't an option. My sister, Marcia, was a graduate student and had no intention of giving up her academic career to work in the family business. Meanwhile, I knew how much my father loved the company and how much blood, sweat, and tears he'd put into it. I didn't want to see him sell it. I agreed to come back home and learn my father's job in order to keep the company in the family.

Honestly, it wasn't a hard choice to make. College had been a big bust for me, and there was nothing else pressing that I wanted to do.

I headed back to Livingston to start my new life with the idea that I was going to one day take over A. V. Thomas Produce. I believed in myself and took pride in everything I did, so I knew I could easily learn the business and perhaps even take it to a new level. It was the perfect way to stay busy.

It's important to remember that at that point in my life, aside from occasional college drinking and weed smoking, I had never done drugs. I liked being in control of my life, my energy, and my time, and I knew that drugs would compromise that control. When I returned home, drugs were the furthest thing from my mind.

CHAPTER 4

BACK TO WORK AND INTO HIDING

I left college and headed home, happy to be free of school. Since the age of five, I had been an integral part of the company, working after school and on weekends. I knew how to run the packing and shipping operations and had some basic knowledge of farming. What I needed to learn was the administrative side of running a business.

Our company grew, packed, and shipped several varieties of sweet potatoes, and in addition to a packing shed and warehouses, we had two hundred acres of crops. We'd sell our potatoes to grocery store chains all around the country, and sometimes, when we had more orders than we could fill from our own acreage, we'd buy product from other growers to ship to our customers. I was familiar with most of this process, but what I didn't know about was managing income and expenses. I started out in our accounting department, where I learned about invoicing, bills of lading, and all aspects of funds coming in and going out. I understood how the company made a profit, and I started to see ways in which we could be even more efficient.

After that I moved into sales, where I interacted with our customers, which I really liked. I was outgoing and sociable, so this part of doing business was fun. I knew that if I could establish a good personal connection with the people at these companies, they would continue to buy from us and possibly increase their orders. I also started to see opportunities for reaching out to potential new clients and growing the business, because I was never satisfied with the status quo. In fact, I had no desire to just continue day-to-day operations and maintain the company at the size it was. Besides my work ethic and my desire to expand, I knew myself well enough to know that keeping busy was the key to my success and well-being. Boredom was my number one enemy.

I realized years later, as an addict, that an addictive personality always craves excitement. Some people can just sit home and watch TV or read a book, feeling relaxed and content, but I have *never* been able to do that. For me, routine—and the boredom that comes with it—was a powerful trigger for seeking a high.

When I returned home to run the company, Sandra and I got back together and built our relationship back into what it had been . . . and much more. She was hardworking and ambitious, just as I was. She didn't drink much, smoke, or do drugs, and I felt blessed to be with her again. I had three important things to keep me focused: Sandra, my work, and my car. These were the three loves of my life. The future was going to be awesome.

I started out living with my parents, but eventually they let me move into a little house they owned in the middle of one of the sweet potato fields. This gave Sandra and me the privacy and freedom we wanted. It was wonderful, and we spent as much time together as we could. She was an amazing person who truly loved me, and I couldn't imagine my life without her. It was the kind of love that made me look at her and think she was the most beautiful girl in the world. I would have done anything to show her how much I loved her; I literally would have killed anyone who hurt her. She was my everything. I wanted to spend the rest of my life with her, believing that nothing could ever come between us.

At age twenty, maybe I was a little idealistic, but to me, Sandra seemed perfect.

Although Sandra was the first love of my life, there was a second love too . . . that 1971 Porsche 911. I continued to tinker with the engine and the stereo and enhance the look of the car. Because of the lowrider culture in my area, I also added Triple Gold Dayton spoked rims and hydraulics, uncommon on a Porsche. I had to custom-fit everything, because no one had ever done anything like that to a Porsche. Once the conversion was done, I entered it in lowrider car shows and always won, because the car was truly unique. I even made it into *Lowrider* magazine in October of 1992, and a full feature article was written about me in the May 1993 issue. Later that year, I won first prize in my division at the Las Vegas Super Show, which was the top lowrider show at the time.

Between working on the car and driving it to shows, my hobby took up a lot of time, but it still wasn't enough for me. I wanted to make a difference in the car-club community, too, so I started the Players Car Club. It was basically a group of guys who'd get together to talk about cars, work on cars, attend car shows, and cruise the streets of downtown, which was a primary source of entertainment and socializing for us in those days. I used my experience running organizations and events to get the group off the ground, and we did some very cool things together.

Do you see a pattern developing here? The need to be constantly occupied and seek bigger and better diversions? I was obsessed with fighting off routine and monotony, a compulsion that started in high school and continued after college. I didn't know it then, but the sense of being bored—the dreaded feeling of being uncomfortable with quietness and downtime—is a known risk factor for addiction. But I had no idea. All I thought about was Sandra and fueling my adrenaline highs with my car.

During that first year back home in Livingston, despite my commitment to Sandra, my job, and my car, I reconnected with many of my old high school friends. It wasn't long before I fell into the partying habit that I thought I'd left behind in college. Only this time, it was much more intense. After a while, I was smoking weed on a regular basis, carrying my own supply, and even occasionally selling it. It had become a normal part of my day-to-day existence, and I was high all the time when I wasn't at work or with Sandra. I was also smoking cigarettes, which Sandra hated. Feeling guilty, I'd quit for a while, trying to make her happy, but it never lasted. I'd start up again, and we'd fight about it all the time.

Then I made the biggest mistake of my life.

At first, when partying with my friends, I would primarily stick to weed, but every once in a while, if a different drug was available, I'd give it a try. Why not? It was the weekend; I'd worked hard all week, and I wanted to enjoy my free time. Also, I have to say that trying hard drugs was more tempting and made easier by the experiences I had had hanging out with Doug. He had encouraged experimentation. Now, because I was restless, I was definitely susceptible to trying something new.

Again, the pattern was making itself evident . . . I *hated* being idle. Free time made me uncomfortable. I didn't feel content unless every second was filled up with something new and exciting.

Just one, I would tell myself. *Just tonight.* Famous last words.

There were always drugs being passed around for free, so it wasn't necessary to buy anything. At least not at first. I don't remember exactly how it started, but at one party I asked, "Hey, can I buy some of that to take with me?"

"Sure," my friend said. That easily, I made my first drug purchase.

After that, if I tried a drug I liked, I would just buy some. Having a variety pack on hand was great for deciding which kind of high I wanted based on what I wanted to do that night. Each drug gave me a different kind of high and lasted a different amount of time. Weed was good for relaxing, mellowing out, listening to music, and kicking back. Crystal meth was just the opposite, giving me boundless energy but without any euphoria. Smoking and snorting cocaine was stimulating, energizing, *and* euphoric.

By that time, I had placed a small safe, which I called my "party safe," in the bedroom of my house. When I bought drugs, I would go home and lock them inside it. Then when Friday night came, I would pick the drug I wanted and take it with me. At first, I'd go back and forth between the various drugs in the safe, and when I ran low on one of them, I would buy more. After a while, though, I noticed that I kept reaching for one particular kind of drug and leaving the rest behind. That drug was cocaine. My drug of choice.

Think of it in terms of food. If you buy a variety of snacks but keep going back for the same one, and it always runs out first, then it's easy to identify your favorite. That's the way it works with drugs. I was buying a variety of "drug snacks," and without thinking about it, I found my favorite and eventually stopped buying the others.

At first, I only partied on the weekends. This is the way it starts with most addicts, whether your drug of choice is alcohol or something much harder. It's a progression.

I would use drugs Friday night through Saturday night or early Sunday morning, then get clean so I could go to work on Monday. I really did care about my job and what I was doing, and I knew even then that to do my best, I could not be high at work. But as I descended further into addiction, I didn't want the party to end, so I started getting high on Sunday nights, too.

Oh, shit, it's two in the morning! I'd suddenly realize.

I couldn't go to work still high, so I'd call and tell people who worked in the office that I was going to be late. Eventually, I figured I'd pretty much wasted the whole day anyway, so I'd call in sick and party on Monday, too. But then I'd end up calling in sick on Tuesday. Every once in a while, I'd try to work while still high, but I'd end up leaving. I couldn't do my job—at least not do it right—when I was wasted. It still mattered to me that I performed well at work.

Secrecy and shame are typical for any addict, which is why one of my primary concerns was to make sure nobody knew I was using. If I went in high, the staff or my dad might figure it out, and that possibility kept me in a state of constant stress and worry. I eventually started missing more work during the week, using the excuse that I was not feeling well. This let me off the hook, which freed me to party nearly every night. Thus began my descent into the situation where drugs were controlling me instead of the other way around.

Sandra trusted me and loved me so much that it was easy to hide my drug use, or so I thought. She kept busy with school and her job and didn't make many demands on me, so I was able to hang out with my partying friends without making her too suspicious. But after a while, the drugs, the stress of trying to hide it, and the fact that I had stopped eating properly caused me to lose a lot of weight. In fact, I was so thin and sickly that I looked like a skeleton, and my family thought I might have AIDS! They never considered that drugs could be the problem because I was an overachiever and was such a good kid in high school. My drug use was a total secret to them.

However, the excuse of not feeling well wore thin after a while, especially with Sandra. She knew me better than anyone, and she knew I wasn't physically ill. As much as I tried to hide it, my drug use soon became obvious to her.

At first, she would still come over and sometimes even spend the night with me. When she did, I would do anything to stop my heart from racing so I could sit down and watch TV with her or lie down and sleep next to her. It wasn't like it had been hours since I did drugs. Instead, I might have just done a line a moment before she arrived and been high as a kite. But I had to act normal. Sometimes I'd manage to lie down with her, but I was so wired that I couldn't keep still. I'd go to the kitchen, pound some beer, drink some wine, then take some NyQuil, sleeping pills, or anything else I had on hand to try to come down from the high. It's a miracle that combining all those drugs didn't kill me.

Sometimes Sandra would realize I had gotten up, and sometimes she wouldn't. When she did, it often led to intense fights. She would plead and cry, begging me to tell her what was wrong, confronting me about my behavior, and asking me if I was using drugs, but I never confessed. I just shut down and ignored her.

My weight loss got even worse, making it harder to hide the true reason it was happening. I was ashamed of my addiction, but I felt helpless, unable to do anything about it. I didn't know how to stop, and by this point, I really didn't want to. I lived in two conflicting realities. In one, I wanted to make Sandra happy and do well at my job. But in the other, drugs were the only thing I lived for, and I needed them more than work or family.

Knowing that I would eventually get caught, I stopped going to work. It was too risky. The days of calling in sick turned into weeks, and soon I wasn't working at all. Other than going out to get more drugs or to party, I ended up staying locked in my house *for what had to be close to an entire year.*

Things had gone from bad to worse, and now they were all bad.

CHAPTER 5

THE COVER OF DARKNESS

At this point, just a few years after I returned from college, I was full-on addicted to drugs and basically hiding from the world. I didn't want people to see me when I was high because they would no doubt try to get me to quit. I was using all the time and had no intention of stopping. I basically locked myself in the house and did drugs every day. It was as if I said, "Screw it all," and just gave in to the addiction. That was it. I was a full-blown addict.

This meant I didn't go outside during the day, and I even became paranoid about it. My house had a basement that I'd converted into a living room—what you might call a man cave—and that's where I spent the majority of my time. However, there was no way to get down there from inside the house. The entrance was through a door outside that led down a steep set of stairs to the room below.

What if someone is watching me? I thought. *I don't want anyone to see that I'm using when I go outside to get downstairs.*

That's part of what drugs do to you. They trigger paranoia. Of course, no one was watching my house, and no one would be able to see if I was using during the ten seconds it took for me to get from my front door to the side door. Maybe I was afraid if people saw me walking around outside, they would do something that would stop me from using. I became so focused on not wanting to get caught that I devised a crazy solution.

One night I grabbed a circular saw and cut a hole in my laundry-room floor, turning it into a kind of trapdoor, a secret entrance.

Then I put a ladder through the hole so I could climb down. I could get to my basement without going outside. I'd solved a problem that wasn't even a problem. That's what drugs can drive you to do.

During this period, my parents had gotten used to the idea that I wasn't reliable. Since I was technically still in training and not an indispensable employee, when I stopped showing up, they found someone else to do my work. Fortunately, because I'd always been so good at saving money, I could get by without a paycheck and live on my savings.

The cover of darkness was my best friend, second only to my drugs. I never left the house unless it was at night, when everyone else was sleeping. The only people awake at 1:00 a.m. or later were drug users, criminals, and folks like me who were using the night to hide their secrets. My dealers came by to see me at night. I had plenty of money, so I was never without cocaine. I was a daily user. When I ran low, I just called for a resupply, and someone would deliver it. It was like ordering pizza. I never had to moderate my drug use or worry about making my supply last, because I knew I could always get more.

Even though I had become a loner, I still had a loyal group of party friends who would come over to my place, and sometimes—after dark, of course—I'd go to their houses, too. On nights when there was nobody around to party with, or if I was bored with the party scene, I would get in my truck and drive. These were some of my favorite times, because it helped with the boredom and agitation, at least for a little while. Ever since I was sixteen, when I became legally able to drive, I cruised around without a destination. Sometimes I would just drive along the back roads looking for new places to go and adventurous things to do.

Occasionally, during the day, a knock would come at the door, and it was usually a family member wanting to check on me. I would ignore it when I could, hoping that person would just go away. But people were often persistent. After all, they were worried about me, yet they didn't realize that drug use was the problem. That just wasn't the Carlos they knew.

If one of them had seen through my "sickness" at that point and tried to force me to get clean or go to rehab, I probably would have run away to a place where nobody knew me, just so I could still do drugs. Nothing ever had the hold on me that cocaine did, and I would do almost anything to keep the party going.

I had a mirror-topped coffee table, and my friends and I would lay out gigantic lines of coke from one side of that table to the other. The amount of cocaine I used was so huge and so endless that it would often get to the point where I couldn't snort it anymore. My nose would start bleeding, or it would be so stopped up that I could hardly breathe, let alone get anything up into it. From time to time, I would cough up blood, but even that didn't stop me. Nothing did.

To give my sinuses a break, I knew I needed to stop snorting the coke, and it was then that I remembered how Doug had taught me to make rock cocaine using the baking-soda-and-scouring-pad method. But I quickly learned there were better ways to make cocaine smokable.

The first technique I used involved buying one of those old-style air fresheners, the ones that came in a glass tube. I would empty out the liquid scent and pull out the cloth that was inside. Then I would clean out the glass tube really well. Once everything was clean, I would drop powdered cocaine into it mixed with baking soda and water, then use a lighter to heat it up, much as Doug had. I would swirl the water around while continuing to heat it. Once it became a gel, I would cool the glass tube using ice water. The gel would become a rock. This produced a much bigger and better rock than using a spoon.

But those rocks took a long time to make, and they were too small for my purposes. I was constantly making batch after batch. I wanted larger rocks, so I soon experimented with another method. Removing the end from a tubular lightbulb, I pulled out the filament and used the resulting glass tube (much larger than the ones from air fresheners) to make marble-size rocks. Eventually I graduated to quart-size mason jars, so I was cooking multiple eightballs (an eighth of an ounce) or even full ounces of cocaine at a time.

I became an expert "cocaine chef," learning just the right mix to get the purest, most powerful rocks. I was still doing lines, but when I couldn't do them anymore, I would smoke the rocks instead. I was also still smoking weed, but less frequently.

Going two, three, or four days with no sleep became normal for me during that year. Sometimes it extended to a week to ten days. The longest stretch I ever went without sleep was fourteen days.

Eventually my body would shut down from exhaustion and abuse. I might be right in the middle of doing a line, or I would have just turned on the TV, and it would be like someone flipped a switch: I would instantly black out. Hours or days later, I would wake up disoriented, with no idea how much time had passed or what day of the week or month it was. I had no clue what was going on in the outside world, either, because I never watched the news or read the paper.

One factor that contributed to this pattern of passing out was poor nutrition—or, to be precise, no nutrition at all. When you're using drugs at this level, your body burns through magnesium, potassium, and all kinds of other substances, leaving you entirely depleted. If you're not replacing those essential nutrients through food or supplements, your body will steal them from wherever it can find them. It burns through your fat, then your muscles, then your brain cells. This is often why regular drug users look malnourished and sick. When I'm in good shape, I normally weigh in at around 185 or 200. But when I was bingeing, I would get down to 165 or lower. During my year in hiding, I was shrunken, just skin and bones. I had no fat or muscle on my body at all.

Physical pain was another factor in my deterioration. The pain throughout my entire body was excruciating when I returned to consciousness after my blackouts. Lack of nourishment and being stuck in the same physical position for long periods of unconsciousness would cause my joints to bind up. My hands would almost be paralyzed, and I couldn't make a fist without extreme pain.

But as soon as I would do a line or smoke a rock, the pain instantly stopped. My fingers would work again, and my muscles would loosen up. That's another reason why drug addicts constantly use: there is significant pain involved with coming down off the drugs, but adding more drugs relieves the pain. In addition, since you're addicted, you're *feening* when coming off drugs (a word derived from "fiending," which means your body is craving the drug in order to stabilize itself). That painful process affects your mind, your body, and your spirit. Spiritually speaking, drugs become your God.

After a binge, once my hands were moving again, I would notice how dry and cracked my skin was, sometimes to the point of bleeding. I would pour hydrogen peroxide all over my hands to sanitize the wounds, and the skin would bubble up everywhere, as it does when you pour peroxide over an infection. It made my hands feel temporarily better, and that was one of the ways I tried to take care of myself.

Meanwhile, with all my drug-fueled energy, I was bored during the day, and I needed something to keep me busy. I cleaned and organized the house compulsively. For normal people, cleaning might mean dusting, doing the dishes, vacuuming once a week, and cleaning the bathroom. But when you're on drugs, it doesn't work that way. You either completely ignore your house and it becomes a pigsty or you do what I did: clean obsessively, the way I used drugs. If I had friends over, I might have a reason to pick up beer cans, wash some dishes, and generally straighten up. But even if the house was already spotless, I would still find something to clean.

Everything had its place. Everything was dusted, vacuumed, shined, cleaned, then cleaned again. Everything was perfectly organized; my T-shirts were lined up like soldiers. Every bottle or can had its label facing outward. Every paper clip, rubber band, and twist tie had its place. There was no such thing as a junk drawer in my house. The floor was swept and mopped. The baseboards were dust-free.

It wasn't just my house I kept clean. Even on my worst days, I kept my body clean, too. I tried my best to eat when I could and even take vitamins. I wasn't one of those drug users who went on a binge and didn't shower for days. I still had a shred of dignity. But I was unraveling fast.

When I wasn't burning off energy by cleaning, I was either partying or driving around aimlessly. Why didn't I stop using during the day? Because coming down off that high was unbearable.

One thing you have to understand before we go any further: all addicts think they have complete willpower and can stop using whenever they want to. I would hear that all the time from the people I was partying with. It was the same thing I would tell myself in those early stages of addiction. But it just isn't true. Drug addicts are too often in denial.

In my case, I am still convinced, without a doubt, that I am one of those people who has a tremendous amount of self-determination. Anyone who knew me when I was growing up and when I was in high school would have told you that, my parents included. Even those who know me now would attest to my having these qualities. Once I set my mind to something, I'm going to make it happen. I can start and stop things on a dime when I want to. If something is important enough to me, I'll achieve it without doubt or hesitation. If I want to make any kind of change, I can and will do it.

But when it came to cocaine, I was completely out of control. I was powerless. I was ignoring everything in my life that was important to me, including the woman I loved so much.

But I could not stop. The grip addiction had on me was absolute.

CHAPTER 6

THE BARREL OF THE PISTOL

"Come on, Carlos, let's go out to dinner and then meet up with my friends for a drink," Sandra would say. She would be all dressed up, looking beautiful, and ready to go dancing at a local club or to hang out somewhere else.

"No, not tonight," I would say. "I'm not feeling well."

"You might feel better if you got out more. A social life would be good for you."

She would try to persuade me to do things with her, like take a walk or go grocery shopping, but I offered excuse after excuse. I knew if I went somewhere with her, I wouldn't be able to use while we were together. Looking back, I can't understand how I was able to fool her for so long. Or maybe she wasn't fooled but loved me enough to give me a chance to fix it.

There were no cell phones back then, but we used pagers. If I wasn't home, or if she stopped by and couldn't find me, she would page me: "9-1-1. Call me." The numbers meant that the call was important and needed a response. But I wouldn't call. I loved her, but I loved cocaine more, even though I knew it was killing our relationship. Eventually, Sandra knew it, too.

"Please, Carlos," she would beg. "We used to be so good together, but now there's nothing left. You're ruining our relationship, ruining our lives together. Please come back to me. I've lost you."

I'm actually a very loving person. A romantic. I love being in love, and I loved Sandra more than I loved my own life. But drugs shut down the loving part of me. I just couldn't do what she asked.

Sandra wasn't the only one I ignored. My non-drug-using friends and members of my family would page me all the time, worried about where I was and what I was doing. When people care for you, you can't disappear for an entire year and expect them to take it in stride. They know something isn't right. I could have turned the pager off, but I needed it for communication with my drug dealers and party buddies. Plus, I think down deep inside I needed to know when family members wanted to hear from me. I felt incredibly guilty avoiding them. It was a stressful time.

It's important to note here that as I got more involved with drugs, the people I called friends slowly drifted into two groups. My drug friends were on one side, and on the other side were the "clean" friends I'd known since childhood, including Brian and Joe, who'd been my best friends since third grade. They were the ones who'd come looking for me when I disappeared. They cared about me and always tried to help. But I was totally screwed up and let them down more times than I can count.

Many nights Sandra and my friends would drive around looking for me in all the places where they thought I might be, but I was nowhere to be found. They'd send page after page, and sometimes I would respond just to let them know I was alive. But I'd keep the calls short so they couldn't tell how high I was. My mom learned quickly to be satisfied with those brief calls, because she knew I wasn't going to sit still for a lecture. She'd thank me for calling and tell me how relieved she was just to hear my voice.

Sandra also learned not to expect much from me, so she got into the habit of going out with her friends, and she began to build a separate life for herself. When I was home alone, I'd put on some music that we both liked, which made me think about our relationship and how much I missed her. I had no idea how to connect with her at that point. I had a shelf in the living room with photos of us on it, surrounded by a bunch of candles. Sometimes I would light those candles and think about her, and in some weird way, I hoped this form of "prayer" would heal things between us. Anything other than confronting the truth. For me, the drugs were far more powerful than prayer.

One night, Sandra came by to make yet another attempt at pulling me out of the dark, lonely world I inhabited. As usual, she asked me to go out somewhere with her, and I don't remember what excuse I used not to go, but she left without me.

I shook my head as I closed the door. I couldn't believe what I was doing to myself and what the drugs were doing to me. I knew if I didn't change, I would lose her—if I hadn't already.

I lit the candles in the living room, put on our favorite music, and chose a picture of her from the shelf. Then I grabbed my Glock .45 and carried it and the picture to the kitchen table.

I sat down in one of the chairs and stared at the photo. I picked up the barrel of the pistol and tapped it against the side of my head.

"C'mon, Carlos, come on," I said out loud to myself. "Figure this out."

Tap-tap-tap.

I closed my eyes and inhaled the scent of the candles. I could hear the music playing in the background. I knew I was a loser and felt even more depressed than usual.

I also knew I had a choice to make.

If I didn't give up the drugs, I was going to lose the love of my life and maybe even my life itself. No matter how hard I tried, how bad I wanted it, I could not control my addiction.

The other option was to just end it all right then. I could pull the trigger and stop the suffering—my own and the suffering I was causing everyone around me. I was hurting Sandra, my friends, and my family, and I knew it. It never occurred to me that my suicide would hurt them even more.

I tapped the barrel on my head again and again, feeling the metal against my hair and skin.

Should I do it? Is this really the answer? I kept asking myself.

But I wasn't ready for such a drastic solution. I didn't want my life to end that way. I got up, put the gun away, set the photo back in its place, and blew out the candles. I don't remember the rest of that night, but I probably just hung out with my drug crowd and got as high as I possibly could.

You'd think that the risk of losing the love of my life would have been enough to turn me around. It wasn't. Cocaine had an incredible hold on me, and when I was in the grip of it, nobody could tell me what to do.

I did try. In fact, I was about to make what would be the first attempt of many to quit.

I hid and denied my drug use as long as I could, but eventually word got out, and my parents and friends found out that I wasn't sick, at least not in the usual way. I had always been very careful because of my desire to avoid getting caught. When I used, I would always be sure to put my drugs back in the safe. One day I got sloppy and for some reason hid drugs in my sock drawer.

I'd arrived home after several days of partying and had passed out on the couch, not thinking about where I'd left my drugs or even considering the possibility that someone might find them. Sandra had a key to my house, and when she stopped by and didn't get an answer to her knock, she came inside.

When she found me passed out on the couch, she looked around, probably knowing I had been using even before she found the evidence.

She shook me awake, and somehow I came to.

"Carlos, what *is* this?" she asked, pointing to the bag of coke she'd discovered and tossed on the coffee table. She had searched the entire place and found the drugs in my sock drawer.

I wasn't sure what to say. I looked at her, at the sadness and anger on her face, and at the bag on the coffee table. There was no use denying it.

"I've suspected for a while now, Carlos. You know that. Now this is proof. What excuse are you going to make?"

I nodded guiltily. "I'm sorry."

"You're sorry? Really? Well, I'm sorry, but that isn't enough. This has to stop. I'm not keeping this a secret, Carlos. I'm telling everyone. Maybe if you don't care about how this affects me, you might care about what it's doing to your parents."

I knew I couldn't run anymore. I was caught.

"You're telling everyone?" I asked.

"Your parents. Your friends. You've been lying to all of us."

"Okay, okay. I'll get help," I told her. "I'll go to rehab. I'll do whatever you want."

I was desperate not to lose her, so I did what she asked.

I enrolled in my first rehab at Central Valley Recovery Center, in Ceres, California. Sandra had indeed called my family, and I'm glad she did, because they all rallied around me in support. It was a thirty-day intensive Narcotics Anonymous–type program.

To be honest, I don't remember a lot of details from that rehab beyond people sitting in a circle, telling their stories, and holding hands to say the Serenity Prayer. But just as I did with everything else I've ever set my mind to, I gave it my all, honestly trying to save my relationship with Sandra and get back to living the way I wanted to. I was willing to do whatever it took to get clean.

One of the things I learned in rehab is that you can't count on anything outside yourself to change your predicament. No job, no relationship, no amount of money or glory will get you off drugs, because the work has to be done internally. But despite knowing this, I had the misguided idea when I got out of rehab that marriage would provide me with an extra incentive to keep clean. I thought it would help me create change. My desire to keep things intact with Sandra and make a deeper commitment to the relationship should be enough to keep me off drugs, right?

Wrong.

After that first rehab, I convinced Sandra that I was going to stay off drugs and make my life whole again, which of course I fully intended to do. I asked her to marry me. I talked myself into believing that I was ready to be a father and start a family! I knew that if I was going to make a life commitment and make my wife happy, I could not be on drugs. I also knew exactly what changes I needed to make, and I intended to give my marriage and my drug-free life 100 percent of my effort.

In September of 1995, after I had been clean for around five months, Sandra and I got married. Looking back now, I can see that I was not emotionally ready or stable enough to take such a major step. But I was still young and impulsive and determined to turn my life around. I figured as a married man I would be solid enough to stay clean.

We had a full-blown traditional Portuguese wedding with nine hundred guests. My parents, who were relieved to see me happy and clean again, invited everyone they knew, and people came from all over to attend. The wedding was in a Catholic church, and the reception was held in a local Portuguese catering hall. It truly felt like the first day of the rest of my life.

Sandra and I moved into a beautiful new home, one without a drug safe or a hole in the laundry-room floor. Shortly after that, she got pregnant, and it was the start of a new life for me and for us. The thought of a wife, a child, and a stable, loving home made the future look hopeful and bright. We had a simple, happy life, enjoying normal activities like going to work, going to the movies, cooking meals together, attending family get-togethers, and looking forward to the birth of our first child. I was making amends to friends and family all over the place, repairing the damage my drug use had caused. I disconnected from my drug friends and reconnected with my clean friends.

Everything seemed to be going really well, and I wanted this period of happiness and drug-free life to last. But it didn't. I don't know what triggered my relapse, and I can't point to one day or one moment when it happened. That's part of the problem with looking back: some memories are fuzzy or even forgotten, especially when your brain is clouded by excessive drug use. I do know that I was always able to find drugs when I wanted them. My drug friends knew to keep their distance while I was trying to stay clean. But they were always just a phone call away if I needed them.

I started using again while Sandra was around four months pregnant, and we had many horrible fights about my relapse. So many times, Sandra would be crying, banging my chest with her fists, yelling at me to stop using, begging me to find a way to quit the drugs and fight for our relationship. She would continually tell me I was better than that. It was devastating to me because I loved her so much. So yes, although we had many horrible fights, one in particular is hard to forget, because it was the first time she seriously threatened to leave.

She knew I had relapsed. How could she not know? I'd stopped communicating with her. I'd go out every night and come home high. I'd miss work here and there. As always, she did her best to help me, trying to make me part of married life instead of a stranger. She brought home books and videos about being a parent and caring for babies, trying to get me involved, but I paid no attention. When I wasn't high or unconscious, all I could think about was getting back to doing drugs.

I don't remember exactly what this fight was about. All I remember is an angry pregnant wife yelling and screaming and threatening to leave me.

"Don't go!" I pleaded.

But out she went. She got into her car and slammed the door. I chased her outside, so angry that I banged my fist on the car, trying to stop her. I tried to open the driver's side door, but it was locked, so I did what any angry drug addict would do. I pulled back my elbow and slammed my entire forearm right through the window. She screamed as glass shattered everywhere and my arm started bleeding. She quickly put the car in reverse and screeched out of the driveway.

I wish I knew what happened after that. Most likely she went to her mother's and stayed there for a few days while I passed out. Or maybe I went off to do more drugs. I can't even remember.

Our daughter, Elaina, was born in December of 1996. I had been clean for a short time just prior to her birth, so Sandra and I were getting along better and felt somewhat close to each other again. It was a beautiful time in our lives, though temporary, and the experience of watching my child being born was indescribable. Sandra was in labor for a couple of days, and I made it a point to be beside her the entire time. We had a scary moment during her delivery when the doctor finally came to see her and noticed the baby was upside down. They rushed Sandra to the OR to do a C-section. I was there with her just a little while later, watching as my daughter was born. She was a big baby, over ten pounds. It was an awesome moment for me, a real blessing.

It wasn't long before I was getting high again, and I recall times when I would watch my infant daughter sleep, feeling overwhelmed with love for her while I was actually high. Because of my drug use, as much as I adored that sweet little baby, I sure wasn't capable of looking after her. I wasn't much help with baby care or any of the day-to-day tasks that Sandra handled. I still lived in my own little selfish world, detached from the people around me.

One day in January of 1997, I came home from a binge, walked into the house, sat down on the couch, and turned on the TV. I hadn't been sleeping the previous couple of days, so when I stopped moving, my body shut down, and I passed out. I don't know how long I was out, but when I came to, there was a police officer standing over me.

"You're awake," he declared. In one hand, he held a bag of cocaine. "This belong to you?"

Sandra stood behind him, and there was no denying it. The drugs had been in my pocket, and Sandra had found them. Not knowing what to do, she told me that she had called my sister, Marcia, who convinced her that turning me in was the best option.

"Please stand up and turn around," the cop said. I did what he asked, and he handcuffed me. I was under arrest for possession of a controlled substance, a misdemeanor punishable by up to one year in jail. It was my first run-in with the police.

As I was escorted from the house, I looked back at Sandra standing there, tears running down her face, with Elaina in her arms. This was a horrible scene. I felt so ashamed. Sandra was heartbroken and disappointed, and I was angry—not at Sandra but at myself, for going back to drugs and jeopardizing our future.

I was also pissed that I'd gotten caught and terrified about going to jail.

They sent me to a minimum-security prison where I was housed in a large dormitory with dozens of guys. I knew it would be best if, during yard time, I kept to myself, didn't make any noise, and didn't try to make friends or enemies. It wasn't what you'd consider hard time, but it was miserable. It gave me a real appreciation for the freedom I had lost. I was only there for a week, but it felt like months.

After that week, I got lucky and was conditionally released into a ninety-day outpatient rehab program. It was a typical twelve-step approach, and I was determined to follow the plan. It started with daily meetings and check-ins and got a little less intense along the way. Unlike my first rehab, this program allowed me to go to work and even go home, as long as I attended the required meetings and followed the rules. If I didn't, I would have to go back to jail.

My dad always let me come back to work every time I got clean, but there were restrictions. He wouldn't let me manage money or have any decision-making authority for the company, and traveling for business was out of the question. He kept an eye on me, and he even drug-tested me at times, though I knew how to pass the urine test by drinking certain liquids that produced clean results and sometimes by paying someone to provide clean urine for me. I was hard-core.

I wanted my second time in rehab to be my last. I finished with the best of intentions to fix my marriage, make things right with my wife and daughter, and never use drugs again. I wanted to be a good husband, father, and business owner. I wanted to be a productive citizen, just a regular guy with a normal life.

But I couldn't do it. I quickly found myself on the addiction road again—this time literally.

CHAPTER 7

ROAD TRIP

Eighteen months out of that second rehab, despite going to the required twelve-step meetings and trying to keep things stable with Sandra by going to marriage counseling, I was once again locked into a vicious cycle of binge-using cocaine. I'd use, then I'd stop, then I'd use again while vowing to stop and failing repeatedly. This was the pattern of my life.

Because I hated being stuck in one spot, one of the things I loved to do while high was drive. I wanted to see new things and new places, but since I rarely slept, eventually the drugs and the sleeplessness would intersect, and I'd pass out behind the wheel. It happened more times than I care to remember.

I'll never forget the time I was driving down the freeway and took an off-ramp. I'd been up for a long time. I remember coming to a stop at an intersection, then *bang*! I woke up and felt the car rocking back after I'd slammed into the side of someone's house. I'd hit it hard, and when I came to and looked around, I noticed that I was surrounded by flowers and plants. I had rolled into these people's front yard, over their lawn, over their flower beds, and into their house.

I knew I needed to get out of there, so I put the car in reverse and spun my wheels, trying to stay somewhat calm and not get stuck. Miraculously, I managed to back out of the yard and onto the street without anybody seeing me, leaving quite a mess behind.

During another binge, I came to a divided highway. I needed

to make a left turn up ahead, but because I had suddenly passed out, I ended up making an immediate left into oncoming traffic. It was dark, so I woke up with headlights coming at me and horns honking because I was driving in the wrong direction. I managed to turn around and head the other way without getting into an accident or getting pulled over.

But my driving adventures were not limited to the highway. I once blacked out while driving through a school zone in the middle of town. I crossed the center line, running into another car. I hit him just right, and it spun him out, sending him spinning across the road. I looked back to make sure there were no kids around, and as far as I could tell, no one appeared to be hurt. I just drove away, again without getting caught—and, more important, without hurting anyone, including myself.

There were many other times when I dozed off while driving. My solution to the problem was to do more cocaine, figuring it would keep me awake—creating a vicious cycle of a cocaine high followed by exhaustion.

Sometimes I was coherent enough to know that if I kept driving, I might get stopped by the police or, worse, kill myself or someone else. When I got to the point where I was that tired, if I didn't have a place to crash close by, I would find somewhere to pull over and sleep it off. That often resulted in bad outcomes, too.

Once, I pulled over onto the bank of an irrigation canal in the middle of winter, when it was really cold. I knew I was too tired to keep driving, so I just stopped. I left the car running so I would still have heat. I didn't bother to check the gas gauge.

I woke up freezing. The car had shut itself off, and the windows were frosted over. I had run out of gas in the middle of the night.

I didn't see any alternative, so I got out and walked for miles through the middle of nowhere to either find some gas or make a phone call. The cold weather had a sobering effect on me, and I started to think about what a mess my life was. That night was a real eye-opener: I saw clearly who I was and what kind of life I had made for myself. I couldn't believe what I had become. At that point, I was too high to go home or call anyone I knew, so I kept trudging through the dark, foggy night in hopes of finding help.

I finally saw a house and went up to the door and knocked, with no concern about waking the people who lived there, even though it was really late—or, actually, early in the morning. I'm not sure which.

A guy answered.

"Hey, bud," I said. "My car ran out of gas. Do you have any? I'll pay you for it."

"Sure. You don't even need to pay. Just bring the can back."

Even at that low point in my life, in the middle of nowhere in the middle of the night, I found a good person who was willing to help me out. I was so surprised. I thought for sure he would have told me to get the hell out of there or made some excuse for not having gas. It gave me faith in humanity, even though I didn't feel like part of the human race myself. I hiked back to the car, got it going, and returned the gas can.

During the times I was back at home, when Sandra and I would argue, I would often get a hotel room in Merced. Sometimes I left in an angry outburst of my own, and other times Sandra kicked me out. One night, we had one of our most explosive fights ever. At the end of it, I was ready to throw everything away. I was tired of trying to keep the right balance between my work life and home life. I was also tired of fighting my drug habit and the temptations surrounding me. It felt like I was always struggling, always fighting something or someone. Often I was fighting several things at a time.

I knew that cocaine had already destroyed my marriage and any progress I had made in rehab and at work. But there was part of me that just didn't care. I was willing to throw it all away. I had gotten to the point of saying, "Screw it," because cocaine was all that really mattered.

In my early days of drug use, if I was ever confronted by Sandra or someone in my family, I would leave and go somewhere else, somewhere I could keep partying and get away with it. This time, I was feeling even more willful than ever. I didn't care if I came back home or not. I knew that if I stuck around, the party would end. I wanted to get away, and the argument was a good excuse to escape. It seemed like the only solution at the time, though I didn't want to go it alone.

I called Andrew, a friend I often partied with.

"Hey, man, what's going on?" I asked.

"Nothing, Carlos—just hanging out. What about you?"

"I feel like getting away for a while. Want to come along?"

"Where are we going?"

"I want to go see the East Coast," I said.

"The East Coast?"

"Yeah. We'll just keep driving until we see water. The East Coast."

"Sure," he told me. "I'm down for a road trip."

"Cool."

"Mind if we pick up this gal I know? We aren't dating or anything, but she would probably want to go, too. She doesn't have anything going on, either."

"Sure. Let's do it."

We arranged a time when I would pick them up, and after I hung up with Andrew, I called my drug dealer.

"I'm taking a little trip," I told him. "Can you hook me up with my usual stuff and some of the stuff I get once in a while? Half of one, half of the other?"

"What do you mean by half?"

"A whole one," I told him. "Just split it up into the two types."

"Sure. Give me a bit to round it up."

"Cool. I'll be by in a bit."

What I'd ordered was a pound of cocaine, half as powder and the other half in rock form. The pound was separated into one-ounce bags, so there were sixteen of them—eight filled with powder and eight filled with rocks. That made them easier to hide, so I stashed them all over my new Lincoln Navigator as I prepared for the trip.

If we had been busted with a pound of cocaine in my car—especially split into one-ounce bags—it would have looked like I was dealing, and we would have been arrested for possession with intent to distribute. But I didn't consider that, nor did I think about the fact that we were taking it across state lines. I just knew I wanted to take a trip. I wanted to party along the way, and I didn't want to run low on drugs, let alone run out of them altogether.

I went to pick up my two traveling companions, Andrew and Rhonda. They threw their stuff into the back, and we all piled into my SUV. We hit the freeway and headed east with the Notorious B.I.G. on the radio, snorting and smoking coke as we went.

Basically, we would drive until we found a place where we could party or find others to party with. Sometimes we would stay in hotels, other times with people we met along the way. We stayed a few days in most places, longer in others. Many parts of the trip were a blur, but I do remember stopping at the Grand Canyon. There was no hurry to get to the East Coast, which was our very vague destination, so we moved slowly. It took us a month to get from Merced, California, to Oklahoma City.

One night I remember driving and being really tired. I suddenly jolted awake to the sound of horns honking and people yelling. I had passed out, and so had Rhonda and Andrew. Our car was on a slow roll, moving down the middle of a freeway at what was basically walking speed.

I panicked and looked for a way out. What if the cops were already on the way? We had a car full of drugs, and we had all done so much cocaine that we would be busted for sure.

I took a hard right through some orange cones, a section of the freeway that was under construction. As I did, the Navigator dropped into an area where the pavement had been removed—essentially a long, wide ditch.

"What's happening?" Andrew asked groggily, the impact waking him up.

"I fell asleep. We all did. I woke up to find us basically stopped in the middle of the freeway. I'm trying to get off the road in case someone called the cops!" I frantically replied.

He looked around. "Where are we?"

"In some sort of hole. There was construction, and I drove into it."

"Well, get us the hell out of here!"

"I'm trying!"

I drove along inside the sunken area, looking for a way out. If I wrecked my car, we would get caught. Suddenly I spotted a little ramp of dirt that looked like it might be just steep enough to pop up the front end and get us back onto the pavement.

"I'm gonna go for it," I told Andrew.

By then Rhonda was awake, too, just in time for the attempted escape.

I hit the gas hard, trying to get up enough speed to jump the ramp and get the front end of the car back onto the pavement. But as I did this, I heard a gruesome scraping sound. I knew I had just ripped some of the bottom off my SUV, but it didn't matter. At least we wouldn't get caught.

"Holy shit!" I said, speeding onto the freeway and blending in with traffic. "We made it!"

"That kicked ass!" Andrew yelled. "Awesome!"

I don't know if it was awesome or not, but it was definitely scary. When you're on drugs and going days without sleep, driving is one of the worst choices you can make. This was only one of the many times when driving high and/or without sleep nearly got me into serious trouble.

Once we got out of the hole and calmed down from our little adventure, I decided to stop at a gas station and car wash in Oklahoma City. We needed to fuel up, clean the car, and see how bad the damage was. We pulled into the self-service car wash, the kind with vacuums and air fresheners, and everyone got out.

I fired up the water and walked around the car, hosing it down. There were some scratches, and the front air dam was missing, but nothing too bad, all things considered.

It was warm outside, and while the others went to grab some snacks, I kept washing the car, first with some soap and then with one of those brushes that gets the bugs and crap off. Once I was done with the outside, I pulled up to the vacuums to clean up the inside and empty out some of the trash we'd accumulated. As I was emptying the garbage, the man next to me looked over.

He was a large guy and wore designer sunglasses, a T-shirt, and cargo shorts. "Nice ride," he said.

"Thanks."

"What happened to the front end?"

"Long story. We had a bit of an accident on the freeway."

"I'm Wally," he said.

"Carlos," I replied, then shook his hand.

"You aren't from around here," he said, pointing to the California plates.

"Nope. Just on a road trip, passing through."

"Cool. Where you headed?"

"East Coast. Me and a couple of friends, just taking our time." I paused for a minute before asking, "Where is there to party around here?"

"I got a place where we can party."

"Sounds good," I said.

We talked a little more, and when I was done and the others came back from shopping, we followed Wally to a pad where some people were gathered.

It was a small home, with one bedroom and a tiny living room and kitchen. There wasn't much furniture, and what little there was didn't match. I noticed as I looked through the bedroom door that the bed was just a mattress on the floor without a frame or anything. I could tell this was a party house, rented by someone who didn't have long-term plans to stick around.

There was a pretty girl there who caught my eye. I quickly tried to figure out if she was with someone. I brought out the drugs we had and started passing them around, and she had no problem joining in. She seemed very confident, like someone who liked to party and knew what she was doing. We had a great time hanging out together and ended up hooking up for the night.

The party we started in Oklahoma ended up lasting for weeks.

But then the drugs started to run low. Being halfway to the East Coast, I couldn't order door-to-door delivery service from my usual dealer. I also knew that although I could score drugs locally, they would probably not be of the quality I was used to. Also, my dealers in California usually let me run a tab and pay them later. I didn't have that option this far away.

My first call was to my dealer back home to see if we could work something out. I had a plan.

"Carlos, what's up?" he asked. "You back in town yet?"

"No. I'm in Oklahoma City."

"Oklahoma City? That's not quite the East Coast."

"Yeah. Long story, bro. Hey, I'm running low. Can you send me something?"

"How we gonna do that?"

"Hide it in something so it won't be obvious. Go somewhere to ship it and make up a fake return address. Use my name and send it to my attention at a local hotel. If it never makes it or we get caught, you'll get paid either way, and I won't tell them where it came from."

"Sounds good."

I found the address of a hotel not far from us and gave it to him, and a few days later the package arrived. Sitting outside the hotel, we were all a little nervous about going in to pick it up.

"What if they know what's in it?" Andrew wondered.

"What if the cops or, worse, the DEA are in there waiting for us?" Rhonda asked. "Sending drugs by US mail is a federal crime."

"Whoever goes in risks getting busted," I said. "But someone has to do it."

"Screw it. I'll do it," Andrew said.

He took my ID, went in, and came back out with the box.

"Hey, man, they didn't even check my ID!" he said.

"Hell, yeah!" I said.

We opened the box as if it were Christmas and found stuffed animals full of drugs, a total of half a pound of coke. We knew we were set for a while.

I didn't mind supplying the drugs as long as my fellow partyers did those drugs with me. My only rule was that the drugs didn't leave the scene. They were mine, and they stayed with me. Otherwise it would be stealing.

But because there were so many people, we quickly ran low again. Luckily, our local connection, Wally, knew where to get some.

"It's a sketchy area," he told me. "But you'll be all right."

Andrew and I went to the place Wally directed us to. I kept my Glock handy, ready for trouble.

We scored the drugs with no problem but soon ran out again, so we returned to get more. It wasn't easy to find drug dealers who would trust a couple of unfamiliar guys trying to score a large amount of cocaine, especially rolling through the neighborhood in a brand-new Lincoln Navigator.

One time we got some product from a dealer there but quickly discovered that it was cut with something really bad.

"I'm gonna go get my money back," I told Wally.

"Get your money back?" he said with a laugh. "You didn't get that stuff at Walmart. You can't just go return it."

"I don't care. I'm not paying for bad product," I told him.

Andrew and I returned to the neighborhood, searching for the guy who had sold us the bad drugs. It seems crazy now, but at the time it made perfect sense to my drug-drenched mind. It took some time, but we finally found the dealer walking the streets. We rattled him up some, trying to get him to confess that he sold us bad drugs, insisting that we wanted our money back. He kept denying it, and we realized that our efforts were going nowhere. I ended up throwing the bag of bad drugs in his face, and we moved on. I wasn't going to do something stupid to get us in any big trouble. But if it had been up to Andrew, things would have gotten much more violent. In the end, we wound up finding another dealer to buy from.

Eventually the drugs started to run low again, but this time, my money was almost all gone, too, so our options were looking pretty bleak. I knew it was time to head home while I still had enough drugs and cash to make the trip. It was time for this party to come to an end.

CHAPTER 8

DITCHING

I didn't want to run out of supply on the way home, because that would be a horrible way to end a binge, coming off of drugs on the road somewhere in the middle of the country. That was a major concern, but there was another problem, too.

I started to get a weird feeling about Andrew and Rhonda. It seemed they didn't want to go home at all, and they didn't want me to go, either, not least because I was the one with the drug supply, the car, and the money—what little I had left. Was I just being paranoid? In the state I was in, God only knows. But whereas Andrew and Rhonda wanted to make this trip their permanent escape, I was finally ready to get out of there.

"Guys," I told them one night, "I think we need to head back."

"Back where?" Andrew said with a blank stare. "I have nothing to go back to. What do you have?"

I shrugged. He was right. I knew Sandra would never take me back after this binge, and I doubted my job would be waiting for me with open arms after I had been MIA for weeks. In my mind, I was pretty much finished with life back home. I had burned through everyone's patience, love, and understanding. My life was obviously damaged. It seemed to me that everything was gone, so why not just keep on traveling?

Yet I still wanted to separate from Andrew and Rhonda before they left me. I had this odd feeling: *What if I run out of drugs and money?* They'd have no more reason to hang out with me. Would they just ditch me? I seriously thought that one night they might take my car, my cash, and my drugs while I was passed out in some motel room, then they'd just leave me there.

"I don't have anything, either," Rhonda said. "I'm having a great time right here."

Maybe I was just being paranoid, or maybe I was right. Either way, I started to feel really anxious and uncomfortable. If I didn't agree to stay, what would they do? I knew it was time to go.

They must have sensed that something was wrong.

"You okay?" Andrew asked one day on our way to Walmart to get some snacks.

"Yeah, fine," I told him.

When we got to the store, everyone got out of the car except me. "I'll wait here," I told them.

But I didn't. This felt like the perfect moment to make my move. I watched them walk inside, and I waited for the doors to close behind them. After a couple of minutes, I started the Navigator, shifted it into Drive, and headed west, leaving them behind. I was going home by myself, and I had just enough money and drugs to make it back to California.

I'd worried for so long about them ditching me, but I had done it first, partly as an act of self-preservation. It wasn't easy, because I had a code of ethics, a kind of moral compass that dictated the way I needed to take care of my drug buddies. I always had their backs, and I expected them to have mine. I took a great deal of pride in that. Bailing on friends wasn't like me. But in a Walmart parking lot in Oklahoma City, I had just broken my own rule. I felt terrible about it, though I thought it was my only choice.

My thinking and judgment were obviously badly affected by the drugs. Maybe I would have handled it a different way today. But when you're doing drugs, you sometimes make the wrong call.

It reminds me of the time when I bailed on my friend Steven.

One night, he and I were both doing Ecstasy and mushrooms, the first time he had tried either. While I felt low-key and calm, the drugs affected him quite differently.

Steven started acting crazy. He was laughing, and he kept falling over, running into people, completely out of control. He also seemed to be having a hard time breathing and was frightening the people around him, making scene after scene. He was even scaring me, and people were asking if they should call 911. Finally I decided to get him out of there.

"C'mon, Steve," I said as I led him outside. He fought me at first, wanting to stay, but I managed to get him out to my truck. We got in and headed home. I felt relieved we weren't around people anymore.

"I need to take a piss," he told me.

I pulled over to the side of the road, still high. I just wanted to drop him off at his place, get home, and chill out.

After he finished peeing, he refused to get back in the truck. Instead, he started acting up again. There we were, on a populated road near Modesto, and he was waving at cars going by, shouting and acting ridiculous. I tried to control him, but he just laughed and wouldn't listen to me. It would be only a matter of time until someone called the cops on us.

"Steve, get in the truck!" I demanded. "I can't get in trouble!"

He wouldn't do it. He just kept acting crazy, waving and shouting.

"Okay, man, I'm out of here," I told him. I got into the truck, and when he still didn't join me, I took off and left him there.

Instead of going home, I went to a hotel room and called another friend.

"Listen—I need your help," I said. "I'm high, and Steve is, too. I left him on the side of the road because he was causing a big scene. I need you to help me find him. Come and get me, and we'll go look for him."

My friend came, and we went out and drove around the area where I'd left Steve, but he was nowhere to be found. Thankfully, the next day, we found out that he'd made it home okay. He some-how calmed down enough to find a pay phone and call someone who could pick him up.

Ditching Steve that night is something I regret to this day. Had I been sober, I would never have left him behind, no matter how erratically he was behaving.

I felt terrible about leaving Andrew and Rhonda at the Walmart in Oklahoma as I headed west toward Amarillo, Texas. As I pulled into town, an unsettled feeling came over me, and I realized I wasn't ready to go home after all. I wasn't done partying, and I didn't want the binge to end. I think I knew that when I finally got home, I'd have to face what I had done, and I wasn't ready to do that. Being responsible for my actions wasn't something I was looking forward to. I had abandoned my wife and baby, my family, and my business. I wanted to avoid the shame of returning to what I had left behind.

Even though I was not yet going home, I wasn't sure I had enough resources to continue the binge. I'd left OKC with basically just enough money and drugs to get home. I was nearing the end of my financial rope, and there was no way a local dealer would give me anything on credit.

You aren't done yet, the voice in my head told me. *You still have a car.*

That's right! My car was worth money! A good amount. I headed for a local dealership that promised cash for cars.

"How are you?" I asked the salesman.

"Good," he replied. "Nice ride."

"Thanks. I'm looking to sell it."

"Yeah?"

"I need to get into something smaller, get some cash out of the deal."

"Well, it's in pretty good shape," he said. "Let's go look at the Blue Book and what I might have on the lot that you like."

Did I make a good business deal? Of course not. The lowball offer he presented was unacceptable, but I was desperate and just grabbed it. I drove away in a little used car that wasn't exactly what I was used to. But this was my new reality. I needed all the cash I could get to hold me over and extend my trip a little bit longer. I just wanted to get the deal done quickly and get back to partying.

I then headed back to Oklahoma City, figuring I knew the scene and it would be easier to score more drugs there rather than starting over in a strange place. But I didn't want to run into Andrew or Rhonda. So, after I scored some drugs, I stayed downtown and partied with some new people. Odd as it may sound, being in a different car helped me feel anonymous. At least Andrew and Rhonda wouldn't recognize me driving around.

It wasn't long before I met a girl in my new group of friends, and we got high together, having a really good time. In typical drug-culture fashion, I didn't know much about her or have any idea where she lived. We just went to a hotel room, and at some point, I passed out. When I woke up, she was gone, but thankfully, my cash, my drugs, my car, and the other things I owned were still there. She could have easily stolen from me and taken me for everything, but she didn't.

It reminded me of my own moral code: I would never take advantage of someone that way, much less someone vulnerable and passed out on drugs. I was kind of touched by her honesty. In the midst of a binge, even after I'd left my friends behind, I had actually met a good person. I don't know why she left the hotel room (probably because I was unconscious and not much fun to be with), but her ethics made me realize that I was a hypocrite about all this moral-code bullshit I was spouting. My God—I'd not only abandoned my drug friends, I'd also abandoned my wife and child! Still, even though my family would pop into mind every once in a while, there were always enough drugs on hand to wipe those guilty thoughts away.

Getting up from bed, I realized I was hungry. I went out to my car, and as I turned on the radio, I heard, "Ten . . . nine . . . eight . . . " The countdown continued into "Happy New Year!"

In my drugged-out haze, I had no idea it was New Year's Eve. That's how far gone I was—totally disoriented, with no sense of time and no concerns or responsibilities. But I had enough clarity to know that I had a good life back home with family and friends who really cared about me. Yet there I was on New Year's Eve, alone in a parking lot in Oklahoma. Even the girl I'd hooked up with was gone. There was nobody left. No family. No friends. Just me.

I thought to myself: *Why am I here? What the hell am I doing?*

But I wasn't quite ready to answer that question. All I knew was that I'd just sold my Lincoln Navigator to get more drugs. I was all alone, and I was basically broke.

As my story proves, the need to get high will make you do stupid things. It's not because you lack intelligence; it's because you're desperate to keep the party rolling.

During that Oklahoma trip, because my cash was getting really low and I couldn't run a tab with any of the local dealers, I figured out a way to get the drugs I needed: I could use my credit cards.

"What do you want?" I would ask the dealer. "I can get it for you."

Some wanted video-game systems like PlayStation and Xbox. Others wanted televisions, stereos, and other electronics. I would then go out and buy all that stuff with my credit cards and trade the merchandise for drugs.

After a while, however, they wanted the money more than they wanted the gadgets. A partial solution was for me to go out and buy a TV or gaming system—or even household tools, jewelry, and other valuable items—then take them to a pawn shop, trading them for the cash I needed.

It wasn't long before pawn-shop owners would get suspicious, because day after day I was bringing in new merchandise and selling it to them, only getting a fraction of what it was worth. Ultimately, I was banned by some of the shops. But my desperation for the cash and the drugs kept me in a state of constant maneuvering.

If you know me today, you wouldn't believe that I would pawn purchased goods to get drugs, but I did. I knew I was getting ripped off, but the need for drugs was just too powerful.

Aside from the cost of buying the drugs, there were lots of other expenses that came along with my binges, including gas, hotel rooms, food, and other charges that quickly ate up my credit limits and cash. I typically liked to stay at good hotels and party in nice nightclubs, which required a cover charge. Eventually, my credit cards got maxed out, and because I hadn't made any payments for months, I couldn't charge anything. Still, when you're high, the last thing you think about is sitting down to pay your bills. My debts would often go to collection even when I *was* attempting to make payments and be responsible. It took a while each time to earn enough money to pay everything back, including the debts I owed my drug dealers. Sometimes on a binge I would even write phony checks. This is the norm: many addicts blow through earnings, deplete savings, and borrow from friends and relatives. But there was nobody I could borrow from at that point—not that anyone would have let me borrow money anyway.

For someone who had worked hard most of his life and saved money since the age of five, when he earned his first paycheck, being broke was a rough place to be in. But I was no victim. I'd put myself in this position because of my addiction, and there was no one to blame but myself. No surprise that substance abuse results in more than health and relationship wreckage. It also leads to financial disaster.

That's where I was on New Year's Eve in 1998—sitting alone in a cheap used car, not ready to go home but not ready to end the binge, either.

As I sat there on that celebratory night in a haze, I began taking a mental inventory of what I had done and what it had cost me.

When you're living the life I was living, traveling around, doing hard drugs with strangers, and driving under the influence without getting enough sleep, it seems inevitable that you'll get caught at some point. Most people do.

Some of those people would call me lucky. Others would say God was protecting me, preserving me for the life I live now. Perhaps God was keeping me safe because He had a bigger purpose for me. Whatever the reason, I was fortunate that I stayed as safe as I did. But there were plenty of rough nights that could have led to my arrest or personal injury.

For example, in my history of actively taking drugs, the banks of irrigation canals were a common place for me to stop when I wanted to do drugs or when I realized that I was in no condition to drive. These canals are usually isolated, private, and far from main roads. There are hundreds of them back home, perfect hang-out spots.

One night I was driving through the rain, and I must have been on a binge for a while, because I was exhausted and almost passed out. I pulled off the main road and onto one of the many smaller roads following a canal. I then stopped the car and decided to do some more drugs.

Finally I passed out with the engine and the windshield wipers still running.

Knock, knock.

I heard the sound and woke up. There was a cop standing outside my car door, tapping on the window.

The windshield wipers were still running, even though it was by then sunny and dry. I had no idea how long I'd been out.

I turned to look at the windshield and saw it was filled with black streaks, almost to the point where I couldn't see out of it. The wipers made a scraping sound as they moved back and forth. I turned them off, then rolled down the window.

"Hey, you okay?" the cop asked. He looked around the car suspiciously.

"Yeah, I'm fine," I said. "I must have fallen asleep."

Where are my drugs? I thought. *Where did my pipe go?*

"That must have been some nap," he said, looking at the windshield. "Have you been doing drugs?"

"No, of course not."

"Mind if I search your car?"

I didn't have a choice. If I said no, he would only find a reason to do it anyway.

He searched my car and searched it well, but he didn't find anything. I was shocked when he told me I could go. My pipe had fallen between the seats, and my drugs were in a semicrushed cigarette pack, which he'd pushed aside as he looked around on the floor of the car. It must have looked like just another piece of trash.

I couldn't believe I was getting away with it.

I cleaned off the windshield the best I could and left, making my way back home.

If he'd searched more thoroughly, if my pipe had not fallen where he couldn't see it, I could have gone to jail for sure.

Another time, before the trip to Oklahoma, I went to visit Sandra at the state college she was attending. I was walking around the campus at night looking for her. Because we dealt with a lot of cash related to the family business, I had a permit to carry a concealed weapon. As usual, I had my pistol under my jacket.

I couldn't find her, so I took off. As I was driving through the parking lot toward the exit, I found myself suddenly surrounded by a dozen cop cars. I had a briefcase full of drugs in the car, but there was no way they could have known about it.

What should I do?

I could have blown past them and tried to outrun them, but I didn't think I would win that race. Instead I locked up my briefcase and turned off my car.

The cops got out of their cars, their guns drawn.

"Sir, put your hands on the wheel," the leader said. "Listen to me, and listen to me clearly. If you do anything besides what I tell you, we will shoot you. I have a family to go home to, and I'm sure you do, too, so do exactly what I tell you."

I obeyed, with no idea why they were so concerned about me.

"Roll down the window, nice and slow," he told me.

I did.

"Now reach out with both hands and use the outside handle to open the door," he said.

I did, then I got out of the car and put my hands over my head, walking toward him exactly the way he said to do. I then knelt on the concrete, and they cuffed me as one of the officers reached inside my jacket and pulled out my gun.

Ah, that's what they were here for. Not my drugs. I almost smiled but didn't dare.

"Someone saw you walking around campus carrying this," the

cop said. "Is there a reason you came onto state property carrying a gun?"

Then it hit me. I was carrying on state property, which my license did not allow me to do.

I went on to explain to him that I had forgotten I couldn't have it there.

"Mind if we search your car?" he asked. They did, but they just moved aside my briefcase and never asked me to open it. I'm pretty sure he believed my story, and for the most part, it was true.

They ended up taking my gun that night and letting me go.

Think about that scenario for a moment. I had been walking around state property, armed with a loaded weapon. If the cops had searched the briefcase, if I had panicked and tried to outrun them, I could have easily been arrested on serious charges rather than just losing my pistol for a week.

In another close call, I was partying at a nightclub in Vegas with a big group of friends. I had with me a film canister filled with Ecstasy, plenty for everyone. I went into the restroom and locked myself in a stall, intending to separate the pills so I could distribute them to my friends.

As I took the canister out of my pocket, I heard a loud bang.

A pair of arms appeared over the top of the stall, followed by a head. It was a bouncer from the club.

He made a grab for the drugs, but I pushed him away, turned around, and dumped the pills in the toilet. I turned back around and shoved him again, then flushed.

He banged through the door of the stall, and I held my hands up.

"What, bro? I don't have anything," I told him.

"You did. I saw you flush it."

I said nothing.

"You may not have anything on you now, but you're out of here."

Another bouncer came in, and they escorted me out the front door.

On the way out I tried to find my friends, to see where they were, but once I spotted them I couldn't get their attention. When I met up with them later, they were furious with me.

"Where did you go with the drugs?" one of them asked.

I told them the story, explaining why I couldn't get back in.

"That didn't really happen," another one of them said. "You just took off to party with someone else or sell the drugs."

It wasn't true. I always maintained a certain integrity when I used with others, and part of that involved sharing my drugs pretty freely. It made me a little angry that they would think of me that way, especially since a couple of them were good friends. As usual, my addiction had created chaos and the threat of arrest, but by that point, it seemed as if nothing could stop me except a return to rehab.

CHAPTER 9

JAIL AND REHAB ... AGAIN

A few days after that New Year's Eve in 1998, I got so lonely that I finally went back to the house where I had been partying with my Oklahoma friends and hooked up with that girl I met with Wally when I first arrived in town. It gave me some temporary relief. But I didn't want to stay there long because I was afraid Andrew and Rhonda might show up. There was no way I wanted to face them.

Late one night, or early in the morning of January 7, 1999, this gal and I found ourselves in my car at a park doing drugs and having sex. Suddenly the familiar blue and red lights of a cop car showed up behind us, and a spotlight lit up the interior.

"Stay calm," I told the girl. "Act natural, and it will all be fine."

She nodded, but I could tell she was nervous.

A cop tapped on the window with his flashlight. "What are y'all doing here?"

"We're doing just what it looks like," I said. "I know we should have gone home first."

"License and registration, please."

"I just got this car—hold on a minute." I rummaged around and asked the girl to help me find the papers. Her hands shook as she looked for them.

"Are you all right, ma'am?" the officer asked.

"I'm fine," she said, her voice shaking.

"Just calm down," I whispered. "Breathe!"

For whatever reason, she couldn't. The officer shined the light around inside.

"Why don't you both get dressed and get out of the car?" he asked.

"Sure thing, Officer," I answered.

As he went around to her side, I took a bag of drugs I had hidden under the seat and slid it underneath the car, hoping he wouldn't see it.

But when he opened her door and helped her out, I saw her weed pipe on the seat.

He saw it at the same time.

"Is that yours, ma'am?" he asked.

She went pale and shook her head.

"Is this your car?" he asked me.

"Yes, sir," I said.

"Your car, you're responsible for what's inside."

In Oklahoma, they have zero tolerance for anything drug-related. He placed me under arrest for possession of drug para-phernalia and took me down to police headquarters to book me. Then the cops tossed me in the county jail.

I spent the first couple of nights alone in my own cell. Talk about grim. There was a small slit where daylight spilled in from a murky window high up on the wall.

I felt trapped and lost. Freedom is one of the things we cherish most, but we take it for granted and don't appreciate it until it's taken away. If you've never been to jail, it might be hard to imagine how powerless you feel, stripped of freedom and all comfort. Most people are free every minute of every day. You can wake up, leave home, go to work, go to the gym, talk to whomever you want to, hug a friend, and kiss those you love. You do what you want to do when you want to do it. Freedom is a privilege.

In a jail cell, you have no choice and no freedom. You also have no identity and no humanity. Other people do not respect you. All you can do is sit there with your thoughts, hour after hour, with no idea what will happen next. It's terrifying.

Yes, I'd been arrested before, but I had been sent to a kinder, gentler place where I shared my living quarters with dozens of other inmates. We had TVs in the rec room and were allowed to go out in the yard throughout the day. This place was very different—harsh, strict, and much lonelier. Back in California, the other inmates were more like me. They were from my streets, my tribe. They felt familiar. Oklahoma was a different culture, and I felt isolated.

Over the next few days, as I was coming down off drugs, I was feening and alone. They let me take a shower each day, and I was allowed in the common area for about an hour, but I didn't talk to anyone. I just observed the environment and tried to think about how I would fit in with all the other inmates when the time came for me to be moved into the general population.

Eventually the guards transferred me to a larger cell, which I shared with a couple of guys who were in there for grand larceny and assault. At that point, I was starving after coming down off the binge. I hadn't eaten right in weeks. Of course, the jail didn't feed us enough to keep me satisfied.

"Damn, I am so hungry," I told one of my cell mates.

"You're hungry?" he said. "I have food for sale."

He pulled up the sheet covering the space under the bottom of his bunk. I saw a ton of snacks stashed there, from Cup Noodles to doughnuts, candy bars, and more.

"You have money in your commissary, man?"

"No. I just got in here. I don't have any. But I do on the outside."

"Bummer," he said and started to lower the sheet.

"You can trust me," I told him. "As soon as I get out, I'll put money in your account."

"You sure I can trust you?" he said.

"You have my word," I told him.

For some reason, he believed me, and I ate what I wanted from the store under his bunk. He ran a tab for me. I was there three or four more days, and the extra food and my cell mates' company made it bearable.

Then the guard came by and called my name out, ready to release me. I had phoned the bail bondsman I used back home and asked him to get hold of my brother, who arrived to bail me out. I was so pumped to be leaving and heading home!

I remember getting all the way to the parking lot, then stopping in my tracks. I couldn't leave yet; I owed my cell mate money. True, that guy was a total stranger, and I would probably never see him again, but I had given him my word.

"Let me borrow a hundred bucks," I asked Rick.

"What for?"

"I owe my cell mate money."

He loaned it to me, and I went back inside to pay my debt before we left.

I couldn't live without doing the right thing by someone who did right by me. A stranger had helped me when I most needed it, and I owed it to him to repay him. I hope when he got the money, he realized there were good people in the world, even among us "convicts."

When I got back home, depressed and broke, I came into an empty house. Sandra had taken everything, every piece of furniture, and moved out. I sat down on the bricks in front of the fireplace, in my completely bare house, and hung my head in my hands. *You wanted a new start*, I said to myself. *Well, this is what it looks like.* An empty page. A clean slate.

Sandra had left me for good. Why wouldn't she?

Among my drug friends back home, word had gotten out on the street about how I had abandoned Andrew and Rhonda in Oklahoma. A friend brought it up to me one day.

"Hey, Carlos," he said. "I heard Andrew is around. You want me to give him a call?"

"Sure," I said. "I need to apologize to him for what I did."

My friend called, and I expected Andrew to show up mad. He had every right to be pissed off at me. But to my surprise, he wasn't mad at all. When he came in, he actually hugged me.

"Hey, man, I'm so sorry," I said. "I should never have ditched you like that."

"I get it, bro. Crazy trip, huh? It's all good."

"Really, I am so sorry." I wanted to make things right.

"Hey, you did what you thought you had to do. No hard feelings."

His forgiveness was amazing. I don't know if I could have been as forgiving if the roles were reversed. We then talked about all the experiences we had during our trip and our time in Oklahoma . . . so many close calls! The drug dealers there could have rolled us or, worse, killed us. We could have been arrested multiple times. But maybe I was lucky. Even when I did get arrested, the cop never found the drugs I slid under the car. But everything I had done was obviously a mess. I'd abandoned my family, partied for months, lost a fortune, broken at least a dozen laws, yet I had gotten away with only one week in jail during the East Coast trip escapade.

Those weren't the only close calls, either. There were dozens of other dangerous situations over the years—brushes with death, run-ins with the law, encounters with violent criminals. Through it all, I felt like I had been blessed in some weird way. How else could I have gotten out of it alive?

Now that I was finally home again, I felt as if I had another chance to clean up my life. My brother, Rick, had come to bail me out, and I will always be grateful for that. Our relationship was a complicated one, and we often did not see eye to eye. Rick had made a number of bad life decisions, just as I had. But as his brother, I had always been there to help him through it, which is what brothers are supposed to do.

This was definitely a difficult time for me and the entire family. Yet I felt some hope. So even though I'd lost my wife and baby, even though I was broke, I was going to recover this time for real. I was going to get clean forever. In fact, I was so resolved to make a change in my life that in April of 1999, I enrolled in a ninety-day recovery program called Narconon, a complete approach to drug withdrawal that uses an amazingly effective regimen of nutrition, exercise, and saunas to eliminate drug cravings. This would be my third rehab.

There are several different types of rehab programs, but Narconon (meaning "no narcotics"), is my favorite by far. It was created in 1966 by Scientology founder L. Ron Hubbard, who conceived a holistic program that would use drug-free treatments to eliminate toxins from the body while also relieving the mental and physical aftereffects connected with drugs.

Most twelve-step programs, like Alcoholics Anonymous and Narcotics Anonymous, talk about the need to remind yourself every single day that you are an addict and powerless over your drug use. You get a sponsor who keeps you accountable, and you can call this person if you find yourself tempted or triggered. You're encouraged to count the days, weeks, months, and years of your sobriety, and you earn little rewards for each milestone—chips or coins that serve as tangible objects you can hold on to as a reminder of your achievement.

I've been to a lot of these meetings, mostly because I was forced to attend them by the courts. Every meeting starts out the same.

"Hi. I'm Carlos, and I am an addict." That's your identity.

Then, in a timed period of sharing, you talk about the depth of your addiction, hitting bottom, how long you've been clean, and how you're recovering a day at a time.

That is the exact opposite of the way I want to live my life! I don't want to be identified as a drug addict, or even a recovering addict, forever. I am a *recovered* addict, completely finished with drugs. I don't want to count how many days or years I've been clean, and I definitely don't want to hear people's drug stories or tell my own over and over again. To me, it seemed as if that approach would keep me from getting better or even make things worse. I found it humiliating to say "Hello, I'm an addict" for weeks or even years. Still, although listening to other people's stories endlessly didn't seem helpful at all to me, I recognize that each person has to find what works best for him or her.

As I discovered, Narconon has an entirely different approach from the twelve-step model. It doesn't load you with the belief that you're an addict for life. Instead, it teaches you that you can get better by learning new life skills, including communication, nutrition, and emotional self-care. The structured exercise regimen was great for me: I remember jogging on the beach, working out in the gym, then sweating in the sauna to rid my body of drug residues. I even quit smoking while I was there and did everything I could to focus on being healthy.

I also really liked the booklets they gave us to read and the mental exercises they offered, which helped us mark new milestones every day. I was encouraged to direct my attention away from past memories and focus on the present and my immediate surroundings. These exercises taught me to be at ease in the moment, to relax and let go of my intense need for constant stimulation. It got me back to reality and showed me how to heal broken relationships. I had to write letters to the people I'd hurt and make amends, asking for their forgiveness, a process that helped me stop lying to myself.

All in all, Narconon teaches addicts how to live. In some way, it takes you back to the person you were before the drugs. You leave feeling renewed, as if drugs had never come into your life.

The program also teaches you to live in the now as opposed to the past or the future. When you're using drugs, the real world continues moving forward, but you're stuck in your own little drug bubble. You're isolated and obsessed, just focused on your next binge, your next high, rather than being part of a community of friends and family. But when you stop after a number of drug-filled years, you need to find ways to get caught up to the world as it currently is. Narconon helps you reset your mentality. Even better, you can leave rehab with the tools to face life without drugs and without the need for ongoing meetings and constant support. Those things are reminders of your past instead of tools for moving forward. I finished the program on March 31, 1999, and was determined to stay clean.

CHAPTER 10

GOING BLIND

I wish I could remember which triggers prompted me to restart my drug use after each period of being clean. But what's the difference? I'm sure whatever it was, it was just an excuse.

Addicts have a way of justifying their behavior, finding reasons to relapse. Blaming others is probably the thing I did most, making it someone else's fault. It might have made me feel better temporarily, but any excuse for a relapse is all BS. I relapsed because I wanted to use drugs. Period. After I completed the Narconon rehab at the end of March, I was back to using by June 12, 1999.

Why do I remember the exact date so distinctly? Because I got arrested yet again.

It was a Saturday, and there were only a few employees working that day at our sweet potato company, A. V. Thomas Produce, which had become one of the largest growers, packers, and shippers of organically and conventionally grown sweet potatoes in the United States. I wasn't supposed to be there that day, probably because I was on a binge and my family knew it. Although I had never stolen anything from the company, they still didn't want to risk having me around, and they certainly didn't want the employees to see a member of the family trashed on drugs.

My brother, Rick, was managing things that day. As soon as he took a look at me, he knew I was using.

"Get out of here, Carlos. You aren't supposed to be here," he ordered.

I ignored him.

He walked away, and moments later the cops rolled up. I ran into the employee bathroom and stashed my drugs in the toilet-paper dispenser. Just as I finished, Rick came through the door looking for me. As I was coming out of the stall, he shoved me hard.

"I don't care what you do with your life, but don't bring it into mine," he yelled.

I shoved him back.

"Get out of my face, brother."

This was not our first physical confrontation. There was often conflict in our relationship. Although we rarely fought as kids, we'd often lose our tempers as adults, the angry words sometimes leading to punching, wrestling, and throwing each other into walls and breaking furniture, windows, and anything else that happened to be in our way.

On this occasion, he went to shove me again, and I grabbed him, trying to throw him to the ground. We were both strong and started wrestling, each trying to get a better position on the other. We banged first into the stall doors, then into the sinks. We hit one of the paper-towel dispensers with a crash that was loud enough to attract the attention of some nearby employees. They burst through the door and tried to break us up, and just as they managed to separate us, the cops walked in.

Rick told them I was on drugs and not supposed to be there, and they arrested me for being under the influence. Fortunately, they didn't find my hidden drugs.

I got taken to the police station, and when the cop sat down to look at his computer, he smiled as if he were seeing something there that I didn't know.

"You know the FBI is watching you, right?" he said. "So why don't you just come clean and tell me who your dealers are?"

I shrugged.

"Just make it easy on yourself and tell us their names."

"Don't even go there. I'm not going to tell you anything."

We went back and forth for a while, and they made idle threats, but I didn't tell them anything. I wasn't a snitch—never have been and never will be.

Was this cop messing with me? I don't think the FBI was watching me, but it was possible, I suppose. I had been buying large quantities from some of the biggest dealers in the area, so the police might have thought I was selling.

Once they released me, I went back to A. V. Thomas, but I couldn't get in. My keys no longer worked, since my family often changed the locks during those years. So I broke in and got the drugs I had hidden in the bathroom. I was a determined addict, and nothing would stop me—not family pressure, not the cops, not the threat of financial ruin, nothing.

My binges would last for varying amounts of time, and between them, I would go back to work and my life would be somewhat normal for a while. Sometimes circumstances other than getting arrested forced me to get clean, at least temporarily. In one case, it was the loss of my vision.

One late night after hours of partying, my eyes started to sting and water, and my peripheral vision went blurry. I couldn't imagine what it could be and thought maybe I was allergic to something, though there was nothing in my motel room that would affect me that way.

Maybe I got some drugs in my eyes, I thought.

I pressed a cold washcloth to my lids, hoping it would relieve the pain. But my eyes kept tearing, and my vision continued to get worse. It wasn't all darkness, like being in a tunnel at night. At first, just the edges of my vision were blurry. But the blurriness got worse until I finally passed out. I woke up in total darkness, unable to see anything at all.

I needed to get immediate help, but first I had to hide the drugs in my room. I attempted to do so clumsily, feeling my way around in total darkness, trying to gather what I had and lock the drugs in my briefcase. I did the best I could, then found my way over to the phone.

Even though I couldn't see, I managed to dial 0.

"Front desk; can I help you?" the clerk said.

"Yeah. This is Carlos in room two-oh-five. I'm having some trouble with my eyes. I can't see anything."

"Is there someone we can call for you? Do you want us to call an ambulance?"

I thought about it for a second. "Just call me a cab," I told the clerk.

She did, and a few minutes later, there was a knock on my door.

"Taxi driver," a man said.

"Thanks for coming," I told him after I opened the door. "My vision is blurry, and I can't really see, so you'll have to lead me downstairs."

"Sure," the driver said. "Take my arm."

He led me to his car, put me inside, and took me to the hospital, where the doctors examined me. A few minutes later we had a diagnosis.

"Mr. Vieira, you have bacterial conjunctivitis, also known as pinkeye. I'm going to get you some antibiotics, and we'll get you back to normal again. But in addition to pinkeye, your contact lenses have somehow slid all the way to the back of your eyes."

"My contacts?" I said. "Damn—I forgot I was wearing them!"

I'd been up for several days without sleeping and hadn't thought about removing them.

"Any idea how long you've had them in?"

"Just a day or so, I think," I answered, though I really had no idea how long it had been. Maybe weeks. Maybe longer.

"Well, your eyes are really dry, and your contacts are stuck to your eyeballs . . . in the back. We're going to have to get in there and take them out."

That's how unmanageable my life had become.

I'm not sure who picked me up after the procedure, but someone took me to my mom and dad's house. I didn't have much sense of time, so I don't know how long it was before my vision came back—at least a few days. I was coming off of a drug binge, so I slept most of the time, only getting up to eat or use the bathroom.

Even though my parents were often frustrated and angry with me, they were true examples of unconditional love. Dad always allowed me to come back to work when I was physically able to, but always under certain conditions, and Mom was always there to take care of me when I needed help. Sometimes I'd stay at their house while coming off drugs, doing nothing but sleeping for days on end, and they'd allow me to do that. Mom made sure there was lots of healthful food available, because I was always extremely hungry after a binge. If I was able to stay awake for short periods, she'd talk to me in a calm, even tone of voice, never pressuring me, because she knew that if there was any kind of blowup, I'd just run off and disappear yet again.

CHAPTER 11

FAMILY TIES

Talking about my parents and the conflict with my brother often makes me think about other family members and my regrets about the way my behavior has affected them.

As I've mentioned, my brother was rough around the edges; not easy to get along with; not always warm, fun-loving, or approachable. During the years of my drug use, he was easily angered, and it didn't take much for him to lose patience with me or with other people around him. I have to say I was different. I was a much more patient and understanding person when life was not going well for him. He, like many of us, was dealing with his own personal issues, but I want to thank him for the times he was at the company handling things when I slacked off.

By contrast, my sister, Marcia, was independent and more intellectual, determined to make it on her own. She left home and went to college, earning an advanced degree in political science and embarking on a successful career as a teacher. When it came to my drug use and our relationship, she pretty much stayed out of all the drama, though she was concerned about my health and the fact that drugs had wrecked my marriage and my ability to function in the business. She just was not going to deal with all the BS that came along with drug addiction, so she kept her distance for the most part. I don't blame her.

Then we come to the subject of my role as a father. As I mentioned earlier, my daughter Elaina was born in 1996. But for most of her life, I was absent because of drugs. There was no way I could function as a father. I was using cocaine both occasionally and on binges, sometimes clean and functional, often not. There was no consistency. At best, I showed up once in a while between binges, but it was infrequent, and I wasn't involved in raising her.

When Elaina was just a baby, as might be expected, Sandra and I finally divorced, and she eventually remarried. Her new husband, Adam, provided a positive male role model in Elaina's life, and I am grateful for that. I did get visitation rights with Elaina once I was off drugs, and I remember that every time I got to see her, I would cry. The way she looked at me crushed my heart. She was beautiful and innocent, a perfect human being. I felt like a worthless loser.

One of the many tragedies of drug addiction is the impact it has on children. It's amazing to know that one in five kids grows up in a home where a parent abuses drugs or alcohol. At a young age, witnessing the trauma of a parent suffering addiction has long-term effects on a child.

When I was doing drugs, I spent time in the homes of other addicts where kids were present. Sometimes those children were painfully thin and neglected, starving because there wasn't any food to eat. Their parents were either spending all their money on drugs or so high that they forgot about feeding and bathing their kids. Once I saw some kids so hungry that they were eating ketchup packets, the only food in the house. The next time I visited that home, I brought them McDonald's. Another time, in a different house, some kids were sitting on the couch, looking neglected and hungry, while their parents were in the kitchen shooting up. Those were not places where I usually hung out, but I have been there and seen firsthand the worst of what drug abuse does to families.

In a way I'm glad I wasn't around that much as a dad during the time I was active in my addiction. I would not have wanted any child to witness my pathetic life on drugs. Sure, I regret missing out on the rewards of fatherhood, but I missed out on *everything* during my drug years. It wasn't just family relationships: it was also friendships, the satisfaction of having a fulfilling career, and the enjoyment of simple everyday things like taking a walk or enjoying someone's birthday party. I was unfit to be a parent or an employee, completely unreliable when it came to social engagements and other commitments. I didn't even show up at the wedding of my friend Brian when I was supposed to be his best man. I was too high to be there. Missing the wedding, not being there for him, remains one of my biggest regrets.

But that was typical of me at that point in my life. I just couldn't show up for the people I cared about most. I made excuses or lied about it, which is something many addicts do, often becoming sneaky and dishonest. For example, when I went out on a binge, I would sometimes rent a car instead of using my own so that if family members were out looking for me, they wouldn't recognize my truck.

Often, when I'd go missing, my mom would drive the country roads searching for me, looking for my truck. I felt awful about it. In the days before cell phones, when she couldn't find me, I would get pages from her—or from Sandra and other family members—frantically trying to find out if I was okay. But I never responded. I was completely oblivious to the needs of other people. My need for drugs was the only thing that mattered, and I didn't want reality to interfere with it.

One of the times when my mother did manage to reach me, she ripped into me over the phone. She didn't ordinarily get that angry, but my behavior had pushed her over the edge. She cried, pleaded, and screamed at me, telling me I was a horrible person for putting my family through this. My parents did not deserve to suffer like that. Nobody does.

Before I got into drugs, I was a good kid, responsible, hardworking, and reliable. That's one reason my parents were so shocked when they found out what I was doing. I was leading a double life that was not comprehensible to them. My mom offered me all the help and love anyone could ever ask for—if I could just accept it. My father was the same way, willing to help me if I wanted it. He had a really hard time understanding the vicious cycle of drug addiction because he was in control of his mind and body, attributes I got from him when I was young, before drugs dragged me into the abyss.

There are some drug addicts who steal to fund their drug habits. I never stole anything—except for the time, in a disgraceful act of desperation, I burglarized my father's safe.

One night, frantic for money to buy coke, I broke into my parents' house, knowing there was a trick to opening the bedroom window without setting off the alarm. I knew where my dad kept his safe, and I thought I knew exactly where the key was. But when I looked for the key, it wasn't there. Whether he moved it or I just remembered incorrectly I have no idea. But I knew I wanted whatever was in that safe.

I decided, in my drugged state of mind, to just take the whole thing! Amazingly, I somehow managed to get it outside and into my car. I then drove to the house of a friend, someone I got high with.

We tried to break into it, but we had no idea what we were doing. We tried a crowbar, a sledgehammer, and a cutting torch, but nothing worked. Finally, we gave up, but I couldn't just sneak back in through the window and return the safe, not least because we had already damaged it. We had to just get rid of it, so we went for a drive and tossed it onto a canal bank.

At some point my father got hold of me by phone.

"I know you took my safe," he said flatly. "I have important documents in there. It's paperwork I can't replace."

I felt guilty as hell already, and he was laying it on pretty thick.

I finally gave in and told him where I dumped it. After that, I never stole from my parents or anyone else again. I was many things, but a thief was not one of them, even when I was on a binge and broke.

My binges, combined with my management style, often caused arguments with my father, especially over the family business. When I was around, I was totally hands-on—loading trucks, traveling with our salesmen, walking the packing line, and trying to improve efficiency. As with everything I do, I would give it my all, growing the business and making the company successful above and beyond what my father or brother thought possible.

Then I would take off on a binge, and my father—or sometimes my brother—would have to step in to run things again, unfamiliar and uncomfortable with the changes I'd implemented, even though they were all positive. That meant more responsibility for my father, which pissed him off, understandably so.

I would come back from those binges humble, working my way back into people's trust and into my former position with the company. The pattern would then repeat itself: I would work hard, grow the business some more, then disappear again.

My father and mother still loved me dearly, and in spite of everything, they would still take me in, letting me stay at their home when I needed help or a place to get clean. I remember one night coming off a binge when I was in my parents' house. I didn't really want to be there, because I didn't want to stop doing drugs. I didn't have a car, so I couldn't get away, and they were watching me to make sure I wouldn't leave.

"Hey, I'm going out back to have a smoke," I told them.

As I stood there smoking, I realized that I could just take off and leave, so I jumped over the fence into the neighbor's yard. I instantly heard dogs barking and felt them biting at my heels. It was pitch black, and I had no idea if those neighbors had a pool or if I would trip over something and hurt myself. I made it to the street, across to a park, then into an almond orchard. I knew exactly where I was headed.

A friend of mine who lived farther downtown always had drugs, so I decided to run over to his place to use. The owner of the orchard must have been irrigating, or maybe it had just rained, but it was really muddy and slick. My shoes got so firmly stuck in the mud that I literally ran right out of them, but I just kept running in my socks!

I didn't care. I was so driven and so determined to get to a place where I could find drugs that I left my shoes right there and kept on going, my lower legs covered in mud. I got to the street and ran without shoes all the way to my friend's house.

His garage door was open, so I ran in and sat down against the wall, trying to catch my breath. My friend, who was partying, took one look at me in my muddy socks, huffing and puffing, and laughed his ass off, wondering why I looked like I had just run a marathon.

I hope that now, after all these years of being clean, my family will understand my intention to spend the rest of my life making up for what I've done to them. I never meant to hurt them. I was hooked on drugs, yes, and suffering because of it. For years, I couldn't stop using, my addiction driving me to behave in ways that went against my personal values and standards. I know the pain and suffering it caused everyone around me. I'm truly sorry and ask for forgiveness. I also hope my parents know how much I love them and appreciate the values they raised me with. No, I didn't always live up to their expectations. But it was never their fault.

CHAPTER 12

TWO KINDS OF GETAWAYS

Months later, I was back at Narconon, my drug rehab of choice, for a second time, though my willingness to stick with the program was not as strong as it had been that first time.

During the first day or so, during the withdrawal stage, when I was still feening for the drugs, I was hurting so much that I decided to leave. I wasn't ready to get clean, it seemed. It was a voluntary program, so the doors were always open if anyone wanted to exit, even though it was not easy to get back in.

True, a night watchman was on duty in the basement, but he was there to make sure no one got hurt and that nobody broke in rather than to keep the addicts imprisoned.

I waited until that guard passed my room on his rounds, then I snuck out into the night. I didn't have a way to get in touch with anyone, so I walked and walked until I found a pay phone.

I needed to call someone who would help me leave rehab—which my friends and family obviously wouldn't do. So I called my drug dealer instead.

"Hey, man," I told him. "I got dropped off somewhere I don't want to be."

"Oh, yeah? Where are you?"

"Newport Beach."

"You know how far that is, right?"

"Yeah, I do. Can you come get me?"

"Sure, man," he told me. "See you in five hours."

He drove all that way to pick me up. What inspires that kind of response from a drug dealer? The fact that I was a good customer. I spent tens of thousands of dollars with many of my dealers, and they would often front me whatever I needed. As any other business owner does, drug dealers take good care of their best customers.

At a certain point, there is a hopelessness that sets in for addicts and the people around them. For me, that point arrived around December of 1999, when my family and friends, tired of all my ups and downs, were running out of options to help me. Sandra was with Adam and was raising our daughter, Elaina, creating a life completely independent of mine. Meanwhile, friends and family had lost all hope of my getting straight over the long term, at least in my hometown environment. They decided to try a new idea: getting me *away* from home.

"Why don't you go with your father to the Azores? Get away for a while?" my mother asked me.

My family owned a place in the Azores—our home away from home. My parents still felt very strong ties to their Portuguese birthplace, which was also home to our very large extended family, including cousins, uncles, aunts, grandparents, and even great-grandparents. We vacationed there frequently, and it was the perfect spot for a getaway from drugs, far away from any temptation. Or so I thought.

I imagined that the trip, in January of 2000, would be almost like going to rehab—a place to get clean, a safe environment with family support. Knowing this trip could help me stay away from drugs, I agreed to go. But I stayed high right up until it was time to leave. Why? Because I didn't want to experience feening on the plane. To make the trip easier for myself, I snuck some drugs through security and onto the plane. This was before 9/11, so it was a lot easier back then.

Once we were on our way, I went to the bathroom to use the drugs, and of course I was in there a long time.

"Are you okay in there, sir?" a flight attendant asked, knocking on the door.

"I'm fine. I'll be right out," I told her.

"Sir, are you okay?" The knock came again, so I finally finished up.

My dad absolutely knew I was still using and must have known I used on that plane. But he believed that I wouldn't be able to get drugs once we got to the islands. He sat back and hoped for the best.

Once in the Azores, Dad stayed busy doing the things he enjoyed or needed to do for himself while I hung out with family and friends. I met new people as well. But it didn't take long before weed came into the picture. I went ahead and joined in, though I stayed away from cocaine and other hard drugs. I knew I could have found them if I really wanted to, but I didn't.

I genuinely enjoyed seeing everyone I met and spending time with my family. It was a relief to be doing normal things like swimming, eating out, enjoying beautiful sunsets, and conversing with healthy, cocaine-free people. The trip was probably the best five months of my life, and for the most part, I was clean.

While there, I became friends with a local guy named Flor. He didn't use drugs or drink much, and he was a good influence on me. We hung out together, driving around the countryside, going to cafés, and visiting with friends. When it was time for me to return to the States, Flor came back with me in search of a better life in America.

When we got back to California, I was ready for a new beginning, while Flor needed me to help him adjust to life in a new country. I got him a job at A. V. Thomas, and he stayed for a while, but eventually he got homesick and went back to the Azores.

Soon after he left, my typical boredom set in, a true danger sign. I went right back into my old life.

A pattern was starting to emerge. When I was in the right place and in the right frame of mind, with enough distraction and stimulation, I could stay away from cocaine. But when I wasn't, when I didn't feel I had a purpose, and when there wasn't anything new and exciting to latch on to, I could not resist the call of the drugs.

How did I get back into it? How did I get started again? Which trigger was it this time? I have no idea. My memory isn't clear enough to pinpoint every trigger for every relapse. All I know is that even when I was willing to do whatever it takes to get clean, the boredom and the need for excitement were just too overwhelming.

By the early summer of 2000, Flor had gone home, and I felt lost, aimless, and quite anxious again. I think back now and ask myself, *Why wasn't work enough to enable me to stay clean? Why wasn't family enough for me?* I know it should have been, but apparently it was not. Although the rationale behind taking a break with my father was to get away from using, it didn't take long until I was back in full force, doing drugs and looking for trouble.

One night, while driving a rental car so family members couldn't identify me if they were out searching, I met up with a couple of female friends who wanted to get high. I had around an ounce of weed and an ounce of cocaine in the car, both stashed away pretty well in case I ran into the cops. I told the girls to follow me in their car, and as we pulled into an isolated spot in an orchard, we parked and got out.

The night was quiet. The spring air was cool and pleasant, and we just stood around talking while we smoked weed. Then we saw a pair of headlights rolling up on us.

"It's probably the landowner," I said.

"Okay. Let's get out of here. We'll meet up later," one of the girls said.

They got into their car, and I got into mine.

As I turned around and headed onto the road, the car that had rolled up followed me. The second I hit the pavement, I floored it, intending to get out of there, not knowing who was on my tail. But as soon as I sped up, blue and red lights came on.

I had drugs in the car. I had just finished smoking weed, and I was already high on coke from earlier, so I knew I would get busted. I pushed the pedal all the way down, going as fast as I could, trying to outrun the cop, but the rental car didn't have enough speed.

I made several turns, but he still stayed with me. I tried turning my lights off and driving faster to try to lose him, but it was too dark and too dangerous to continue this futile effort. I knew that if I didn't turn the lights back on, I was going to crash.

Finally, I gave up and pulled over.

The cop approached the car.

"Get out of the vehicle," he demanded brusquely.

I did.

"Why are you trying to outrun us?" By this time, another patrol car had joined him.

I don't know what bullshit excuse I used, but of course he didn't believe me.

"You were throwing out the drugs, weren't you?"

"I have no idea what you're talking about."

"Go back and check," he told the other officer. That cop started cruising up and down the stretch of road a mile or so behind us, shining his light on the shoulder, looking for a place where I might have gotten rid of something.

But I hadn't gotten rid of anything.

While his partner was doing that, the first cop gave me a field sobriety test, which I failed.

"Where did you toss them?" the officer asked me again.

"I have no idea what you're talking about," I answered.

He put me into the back of his cruiser, then they searched my rental car but found nothing.

"You're under arrest for reckless driving and being under the influence," he told me.

They took me to jail and booked me. They also impounded the car, but they never found the drugs hidden inside.

When I got out of jail, I went back to the rental place to see if I could rent the same car so I could retrieve my drugs, but it was gone, rented to someone on a one-way trip. The drugs are probably still in that car to this day, wherever it is.

Looking back, I'm shocked by how oblivious I was to the dangers of my lifestyle, not only for myself but also for others. I'm ashamed to admit how many times I drove a car while obliterated on drugs, with all my judgment and reaction time completely disabled. Ten thousand young people in the United States are killed every year as a result of drinking and drugging while driving. It's an absolute miracle, by the grace of God, that I never hurt or killed anyone with a motor vehicle.

Getting busted had become a normal part of my life. I was careless and reckless, so naturally I was always susceptible to getting caught. It seemed to happen all the time, almost for no reason at all. One time I was talking on a pay phone outside a convenience store when a cop pulled up. I wasn't sure what I did wrong, but I knew my family had a missing-person report filed on me, so if the cop found out who I was, he would take me in.

"Got any ID?" the cop asked.

"No," I said, which may or may not have been true. Either way, I was not going to give it to him.

"What's your name?"

I gave him someone else's name.

"Oh, yeah? What's your birthday?"

I don't remember if I got the birthday right or wrong, but he must have been suspicious, because he followed up with another question.

"What's your Social Security number?"

I knew I was caught. Maybe the cop already knew who I was. I tried to stumble through the answer, but I clearly did not know the right Social Security number.

"You're lying," the cop said. "You're under arrest for giving a false ID and lying to a police officer."

He put me in the back of the car and took me to jail, where I spent the night.

But even after that arrest, I wasn't done with the police, and they weren't done with me. Six months later I got arrested yet again, this time for driving under the influence. My friends and I had been watching a football game at a local bar and decided to go back to my house. We stopped at a convenience store to grab some snacks and beer, and we were joking around with each other and goofing off a bit in the store. We were probably being too loud, and I guess the owner called the cops. A couple of blocks from my house, a police car came flying up behind us with his lights on. He said he stopped me because he saw me swerving, but I knew that wasn't true, because he'd been behind me for less than a minute.

I spent the night in jail and lost my license for six months. I also had to do a short alcohol rehab as part of the deal. It seemed as if I would never rebound from the life I was living, which could only move in one direction—*down*.

CHAPTER 13

HIGH RISKS AND CLOSE CALLS

I had one party friend named Al who lived out in the middle of nowhere on a farm. He was crazy, a little manic—or at least I thought so at the time—and I never knew what to expect from him. Even when I went to his house just to chill, it was never dull. He made his own excitement.

Al could be paranoid when he was high; he was one of those guys who was on edge quite a lot. Sometimes when I'd get to his place, I'd find him outside shooting a gun just for the fun of it.

One time I drove to his house in a rental car. To get to his farm, you went down a long dirt road, then you arrived at a fenced-off area. The gate was always open, even if Al wasn't expecting anyone.

It was the middle of the night, and I pulled up in front of the house and got out.

"Al, where you at?" I called out.

I heard him say something, but I couldn't understand him.

"What?" I said, then turned around.

I heard a sound in a nearby tree and looked up. He was in the top of the tree and had a shotgun pointed at me.

"Hey, it's me!" I said.

"Who are you?" he replied.

"It's me—Carlos."

"Carlos who?"

"Carlos Vieira!"

"Why are you here?"

"I'm just here to hang out. What are you doing up there?"

There was a long pause. His gun still was pointed at me, his eyes wide open. For a second, I wasn't sure if he was going to blow a hole in my chest, so I just stood there. He eventually lowered the barrel and came down from the tree.

We then went into the house, did the drugs that I had brought along with me, then settled in, hanging out. He seemed fine. But then he left for a few minutes and never came back. I thought he was just going to the bathroom or out for a little fresh air.

I went onto the porch to look for him. "Al, where are you?"

He didn't answer. An odd feeling came over me, and I looked up in the tree to see if he was back up there.

He wasn't.

"Al, where did you go?"

There was no answer.

The farm was dark, with no outdoor lights. The house was dark, too, so only the light from the full moon lit up the countryside.

My ears filled with the sound of crickets until I heard what I thought might be twigs breaking under someone's shoes.

"Al?" I said, more quietly this time.

Something or someone was out there, and if it wasn't Al, what or who was it? I knew that if I got attacked, surrounded by acres of empty fields, no one would hear me even if I could call out for help. I had to get out of that spooky place, so I jumped into my car and drove toward the always open gate.

The gate that was never locked was now locked . . . with a padlock. Someone had come down there and trapped me in. I turned around and drove back toward the house, wondering if there was another way out.

As I drove down the dirt road, all of a sudden truck lights came on behind me. I heard the engine rev, then I heard gunshots. It had to be Al. He was already paranoid, and now he was even higher after we had done the drugs I brought, so his aggression was really ramped up. I had no idea what he might do next.

He was shooting—I assumed at me—speeding right up to my back bumper. I accelerated, looking for an escape.

There was a canal bank nearby, and the road beside it ran all the way around the property. Trying to escape all those acres of farmland was like trying to find a way out of a maze. I figured there had to be another gate, a gap, or some kind of exit.

Al was still chasing me, firing away. Was it at me or the sky? In all my misadventures, I had never yet been involved in a shoot-out. At that point, I didn't know if he was just screwing around or if it was for real. I had my gun on me. But did I really want to shoot back, knowing that I could end up hitting him or, worse, killing him? For all I knew, he was just trying to scare me. I decided to outrun him. The problem was that Al obviously knew the area better than I did.

I don't know how it happened, but I'd gone around in a circle and found myself back at the locked gate. I was screwed.

I turned around, this time headed for a far corner of the property that was close to the main road. I sped toward the canal bank and floored it. My car jumped over the bank, caught air, rammed through the fence with a crash, and landed on the road that paralleled his property.

Al had stayed at the fence and didn't give chase.

To this day I don't understand what happened that night. Was Al really after me? Was he trying to take my drugs and shake me down? Was he on his own little crazy trip? I don't know. But the bigger question is, did I hang out with Al again?

Of course, I did! The drama and thrill of the chase excited me no matter what the risk. I went back there to party many times after that night, driven by my undeniable need for excitement, risk, and unpredictability.

The encounter with Al was not the only time my life seemed to be in danger. Besides dealing with the cops, I had plenty of other close calls.

For example, once I got dropped off at my friend Ron's house to party, and I remember a bunch of guys showing up. At first, I thought they were friends of Ron coming to join the fun.

As usual, I had a lot of drugs and cash on me. I was sitting at the table snorting, and one of the guys sat down across from me. As he did, he laid a gun on the table.

"How's it going?" he said. He slid the magazine out of his pistol.

"Good," I said.

"Cool," he replied.

He popped the bullets out of the magazine, and they clattered onto the table.

We exchanged small talk. I wasn't really interested in having a conversation with him, but while we talked, he started wiping each bullet off with a cloth and putting it back into the magazine. While he was doing this, one of the guys who was with him moved to stand near one of the doors. Another guy moved to the other one.

Something was about to go down. Something bad. They were covering the exits, and there was no way out of the room without going through them.

"You got a lot of drugs here, man," the guy with the gun said.

"Yeah," I said, keeping my eye on all of them. "But not enough for a real party," I added, thinking fast and trying to come up with an out. "We need more."

"You party like this a lot?"

"Sometimes," I told him. I knew I needed to figure a way out of there, and I had a plan.

He just nodded.

"I need to call my dealer," I told him. "These drugs aren't going to last all night, and I need to get some more before it gets too late."

"That sounds good," he said, looking at me. "Go for it."

I borrowed the house phone and called my dealer. I told him what I wanted and where to meet me—a little corner store a couple of miles from Ron's, which would allow me to make an escape. He said he would be there in twenty minutes.

I then remembered that I had been dropped off and didn't have a car, so I turned to the guy with the gun.

"I don't have my car. Can one of your guys give me a ride?"

"Sure."

He nodded to one of the others. They probably figured they could jump me after I had bought the drugs.

One of them took me to meet my dealer at the store. He waited in the car while I walked over to talk to my dealer.

"Yo, bro," I told him. "It is cool I get a ride from you?"

"Where?" he asked.

"Anywhere; it doesn't matter."

He agreed, so I went back to the guy who had driven me there.

"I have to take care of something," I told him. "Tell my buddy I'll catch him later."

"Okay," the guy said. I could tell he was reluctant to go back without me, but I got in my dealer's car and took off.

A few days later I met up with Ron, the guy whose house we'd been in.

"What was up with those guys?" I asked him. "It seemed like they were going to jump me."

"They were," Ron confirmed. "Sorry, man. They said it was either you or me. You know how it is."

I did *not* know how it was. I would never have betrayed a friend like that. But then again, he wasn't me, and this was the drug life.

Still, it didn't matter. Like Al, Ron was fun to party with, so I went back to hanging out with him. The risk was part of what kept me hooked. The guy with the gun never showed up again, but I also made it a point to always have a car with me and my gun close by.

There were times when I would have a lot of expensive stuff in my car in addition to drugs and cash. Sometimes I was taking it to either sell or trade for drugs, and other times I was just moving it from place to place.

I was in the town of Turlock once looking for someone to party with. When you've been doing drugs long enough, you can spot people who are like you—using—and looking to party. I came upon a guy I kind of knew from the past and picked him up. I sensed from the start that he was bad news, kind of sketchy and erratic in his behavior. But I didn't want to party alone, so I thought I could handle him well enough. We went to a mutual friend's house to do drugs and hang out. After some time there, he asked me for a favor.

"Carlos, can you give me a ride somewhere?"

"Sure," I told him. "Where to?"

"I just need to go get something," he told me.

The place he directed me to was in a very run-down high-crime neighborhood, but I was armed, and I figured I could defend myself if something did go down.

It was very late at night, desolate, with almost no cars around, everything eerily quiet.

We parked in front of a house located away from traffic and streetlights. The guy walked up to a door and knocked, then looked back at me. His eyes went from me to a point down the road a little bit behind me. I used my mirror to look in the direction he had been looking.

I saw a pair of brake lights come on and light up the darkness behind me. Even when I was high, especially with sketchy people, I always kept an eye on my surroundings.

I glanced over at the guy waiting on the porch and noticed he had moved behind a post, as if he was taking cover. I looked in my mirror again and saw the darkened car rolling slowly toward me, headlights off.

I brought out my Glock and ducked really low in my seat, sliding down as far as I could and making myself as small a target as possible.

The car slowly rolled up behind me, so I put my foot on the brake and shifted my own car into gear. I was ready to take off at any second, and I wanted the people in the other car to know it.

As they pulled up alongside me, they looked over and then drove off, seeing that I was not the easy mark they thought I was going to be. After they sped away, I sat up.

The guy I picked up came out of hiding and got back in the car. No one came to the door the whole time he was supposedly waiting to pick something up.

"What was that all about?" I asked him.

"They weren't home," he told me. "Let's go."

Despite the fact that he had clearly set me up and was obviously lying, I took him with me, still looking to party. I was not only receptive to danger, I also welcomed it.

That night, if I hadn't noticed the car rolling up on me, I'm sure I would have been jumped. I could have been robbed or even shot to death, the victim of a drive-by. Thankfully, I was watching my own back.

No matter where I went in the drug world, I knew I could be a target. Anyone walking around with the kind of drugs and money I usually carried had to be aware of that. It wasn't like me to be careless, even when I was on a binge. There were plenty of times no one had my back but me, so I kept my intuition on high alert. I guess I got lucky, because there were so many times during my years of using when things could have turned out so much worse.

Another example is when I got set up by a couple I picked up—partyers like me.

"How you guys doing?"

"Good, good," the girl said. She seemed to be flirting with me, and that worried me a little at first. I didn't want to upset the dude if the two of them were together.

"Ready to party?"

"You bet," the guy said. "We don't have any other plans."

In the first few minutes, it became pretty obvious that they were not a couple. She was attractive, and I thought she would be fun to party with, and I saw no reason not to include him.

I opened the center console in my car, which was filled with drugs. His eyes lit up.

"Wow, this is going to be a helluva party!" he said.

"Help yourselves," I told them.

We were driving around, doing drugs together, when he said, "Hey, man, pull over. I have to make a quick phone call."

I pulled over when I saw a pay phone, and he went over to it. While he talked, he covered the mouthpiece and looked back a couple of times at us waiting in my car.

"You want to come party with me later?" I asked the girl.

"Sure," she said. "We can drop him off, and I can grab some of my stuff."

"Sounds good," I said, staring at him. The way he was doing things felt funny to me. Something was off, and I was ready to be rid of him.

After he got back in, he pulled a knife out from somewhere, maybe just to open a bag of drugs, but that seemed wrong. I paid close attention to everything he did while I drove.

As we headed to supposedly drop him off at an apartment complex, I had an anxious feeling. The neighborhood was pretty bad, and the apartment they were going into faced the back of the property, away from the road.

I pulled into the lot, facing away from the building.

"You can just drop me off here," he instructed.

"I'll go grab my stuff, and then we can take off," said the girl.

"I'll wait in the car," I said.

As I watched in my rearview mirror, they walked up to an apartment on the second floor. He knocked on the door. It opened, and as soon as they went in, two other guys came out. They crept down the stairs to different sides of the apartment complex, staying in the shadows as they descended. I switched to watching my side mirrors so I could keep track of both of them. They were now walking fast toward my car while they were reaching into their jackets for what I could only assume were weapons.

As soon as I saw for sure they were after me, I backed out of the parking space and took off. They immediately ran to their vehicle, jumped in, and came after me.

They followed me onto the freeway and kept up with me even when I sped up to a hundred miles an hour to see what they would do. They followed me for miles until they realized I was leaving the area. If I hadn't paid attention, they would have jumped me for sure.

Lots of times strange things happened that could have easily taken me out. One time early in my addiction, I was at home and headed out to my truck. I was carrying a stack of things in one hand: wallet, cigarettes, and such. My pistol was balanced on top of the stack. My other hand was holding the truck keys.

As I walked toward the truck, the gun just went off, all by itself. I didn't touch it, and my finger wasn't near the trigger, so there was no way I accidentally fired it. Fortunately, the barrel was pointed in the other direction—at the truck, not at me—so it blew a hole in the driver's-side door. If the barrel had been pointed my way, I would have shot myself and been lying there in my driveway all night.

There were many other wrong turns and bad decisions, too, all fueled by my addiction. Even now, reflecting back on those years is scary. What could have happened?

One guy I used to party with got mixed up with some bad people and ended up killing a guy over drugs. He was sent to prison for more than twenty-five years. I partied with a couple of people who were killed over unpaid drug debts, I heard, and I could have easily been with them the night of the murders.

Any one of these things could have happened to me along the way. True, I was always cautious, and I never screwed anyone over. But when you're in that life, anything can happen.

Did I survive because of my smarts or because I was plain lucky? Or was it God watching over me, protecting me? Whatever the case, I feel truly blessed to have made it through those situations.

CHAPTER 14

LET'S GET SERIOUS

At the end of 2000, my dad took off again for the Azores to help build a community hall in the village where he grew up. He left me in charge of the company in his absence, giving me the freedom to do what I pleased without his oversight.

That put a lot of responsibility on me, which was actually just what I needed. I had always thrived on having a purpose, and I liked being in charge of A. V. Thomas, feeling a sense of independence. With my dad gone, I had the freedom to grow the company without pushback, so this was exactly the diversion I needed. I wanted to make it work, and I knew that to make this plan successful, I could not be using cocaine.

I remember telling myself, *I don't need to go to rehab to get cleaned up. I'm not going to learn anything else there. I know what I need to do. Let's get serious.*

I decided to stop on my own. But I knew that in order to stay clean and jump into running the company 100 percent, I would need a lot of self-discipline. I'd tried getting clean many times and had failed. This time, I sincerely hoped it would be different because of the freedom I had.

My dad was happy with the company's status quo. A. V. Thomas was a manageable size, and although we were expanding, the growth rate was slow, which kept things stable. But I wanted to grow it faster and bigger. I knew how to do it.

First of all, I knew I needed to spend a lot of time in face-to-face meetings with customers, which required me to travel much more than I ever did before. Meeting clients in person helped build relationships, and those relationships resulted in more business from our existing customers and helped us onboard new clients. Creating bonds of trust helped all parties involved.

I also built relationships with the farmers in town so that we had more product to sell. They were grateful for the business. What I was doing created a positive result for everyone—our customers and the local economy.

Soon we were growing so fast that I could no longer oversee everything myself, so I hired additional staff. While my father had always been a micromanager, my management style was more relaxed, and I felt ready to delegate more. That was the only way we could grow. So rather than keep tabs on every little thing, I allowed people to own their jobs and take responsibility for their work. It helped them feel more motivated and take pride in what they were doing. I might not be the most educated person when it comes to college degrees, but when I'm making a deal or running a business, I'm in my element. Of course I knew our business from top to bottom and was confident that I could take the company to new heights.

As a result of these changes, the business was transforming at a steady rate. In 2001, I started creating alternatives to the traditional forty-pound boxes that everyone else in the industry packaged their sweet potatoes in. This enabled us to sell to clients who had not previously been buying their sweet potatoes from California. By 2004, we'd launched the sweet potato bag program, an alternative packaging option. We ended up creating an entire product category for these bags, the first of its kind for sweet potatoes. We also developed microwavable sweet potato packs and arranged to be the supplier for the company that pioneered the popular concept of those delicious sweet potato fries. Even though we'd been farming organically since 1988, we created a specialty organic line, which was a big success, along with all kinds of other new packaging options and product lines that separated us from the competition.

In addition to overseeing product development, I made changes to our staff. I created new jobs, grew departments, and moved people around to different positions so that our workflow could be more efficient. I'd previously spent a lot of time on the production floor, loading trucks, walking the packing line, and engaging with the employees. But now that we'd grown so much, I had to delegate those duties to other managers so I could be in the office as well as travel to meet with clients. I had to be free to see the big picture and plan the future innovations that would eventually take the company to unsurpassed heights.

Even though I was heavily involved in the family business and stayed busy enough to avoid cocaine, I was still using other party drugs from time to time. I sometimes used weed, alcohol, Ecstasy, and mushrooms. But this was only on the weekends and only when I went to parties or to the city. I stayed away from my drug of choice, a boundary that kept me functional.

During this productive phase of my life, I led the company for five years without any cocaine in my system. I was keeping my body and mind occupied enough to prevent me from relapses.

No, I can't say that I was clean, but abstaining from cocaine for that long a period was a huge step forward for me. Because I kept to this resolution, my mind, body, and spirit were in the best shape they'd been in at any time in my adult life. After so many years of using drugs, getting clean, then relapsing, plus all the rehabs and broken promises, I was ready for everything to change, and it had.

Things were going really well with the business, and I was

feeling much better overall, taking good care of myself. In 2002 I decided to have surgery on my nose to repair a deviated septum, which had been a longtime problem. In fact, I'd had breathing issues dating back to high school. I'd broken my nose numerous times playing sports and just goofing off. Naturally, cocaine had only made the inner lining of my nose worse. Coke wreaks havoc on the nasal passages, causing a chronically runny nose, inflammation of nasal passages, nosebleeds, and temporary or permanent loss of the sense of smell. I didn't have those symptoms anymore, but I still couldn't breathe properly. I decided to finally get the medical care I needed.

All this clear-headedness and self-care forced me to look at uncomfortable truths that I'd been avoiding for years. I was still riddled with guilt about all the broken promises to my family and vowed that I would never violate their trust again. I held myself totally accountable for what I had done. I pleaded with them to forgive me numerous times, and they always did, welcoming me back with open arms.

Now, in this new, fulfilling time of my life, I could no longer enjoy getting high, not even smoking a joint. First, I knew that I shouldn't be doing it, because ultimately one drug would bring me to another. Second, I knew that relapsing would cause continued pain to the people I loved, so it was hard to find pleasure in using. Guilt was a great way to stop myself. I was aware of the needs of other people for the first time since I'd started using drugs.

My life was definitely looking better—completely different from the night when I returned from Oklahoma to an empty house. The company was thriving, and my friends and family were happy because I was whole again. Building on that momentum, I felt that I could still do *better*. It was time to settle down and quit the party life forever.

I had loved my first wife, Sandra, dearly. From the time we met in high school, she meant everything to me. But I lost her because I screwed up big-time. There was no turning back the clock. She was gone. I told myself that if I ever found someone again, I would give it everything I had. I would make up for the mistakes I made in my first marriage.

In 2004, when I made the decision to quit using all types of drugs and be faithful to one woman, I decided I wanted to get married, settle down, and have children again. I thought it would provide some stability for me and give me more responsibility. I felt that making these adult commitments should be enough to keep me focused, busy, and away from the party life and drugs.

One night in the summer of that year, I went out to dinner with one of our clients, who brought along his wife, Summer, and her sister, Harvest, a beautiful, smart, and very accomplished woman who impressed me right away with how strong and self-reliant she was. She was in the air force, studying to be a pilot, so she traveled around the world. There was an instant attraction, and soon I was traveling to see her wherever she was. She was different from the other women I had been with—stronger and more independent. We got married on May 14, 2005, after knowing each other for only eighteen months. It was a beautiful, elegant wedding held in my backyard, with 250 people and a live band. I even brought out my trumpet and played a solo serenade for my new bride. We set off on a five-week honeymoon, and soon after we returned to California, in June, Harvest was pregnant.

By this time, I had been cocaine-free for around five years. I still did a few party drugs now and then, but I hadn't gone near cocaine since I took over the family business. Right after my wedding and my decision to be truly clean, however, I started to experience a lot of stress, and with it some additional triggers.

It started when my father came home from his trip overseas to find that he was no longer in control of his company. He would ask people to do things, and they would say, "Let me check with Carlos." The growth I had created did not sit well with him or make him proud the way I had hoped it would. Deep down inside, he wasn't ready to yield complete control. He liked to keep things smaller and more manageable. Or maybe he was happy with the growth but didn't like having less control.

I asked my father to leave things as they were while I was on my honeymoon. "If you want to change anything," I said, "please wait until I return so we can work together on those changes."

But when I got back, Dad had made changes at the company, which led to some heated arguments. He wanted to be in complete control, and he wanted me to step down. He was so discontent that my sister, Marcia, even called me.

"What have you done to Dad?" she demanded.

"Nothing. We're fighting over who is in charge and the direction of the company," I told her.

"Well, whatever it is, let it go. It's killing him. He's angry and depressed."

"I can't just return things to the way they were. We've made so much progress."

"Well, you need to make things right with Dad and give him his control back."

What was happening was part of a long history of business disagreements between my dad and me. For sure, we had different leadership styles and conflicting visions, but it seemed to me that he wanted the company he'd nurtured for decades to be under his control, because that's what he lived for. In a sense, the company was his whole life, his identity, despite the fact that he had mentioned he was retiring several times. I think the idea of losing power must have been terrifying for him, and I understand that. The years of my drug use and relapses did not help the situation, either. But from my perspective, I needed to run the company in order to keep myself clean. Our two goals were in direct conflict, though we had one thing in common—the need for control.

The fact was, there could only be one boss. To stay off drugs, I needed consistent responsibility, taking care of something larger than myself. After all, lots of people were counting on me, and it meant a lot to me to keep them happy. No question, they were keeping me happy by unknowingly keeping me away from cocaine.

Before my father went on his five-year trip, I knew that if I took off on a binge, he would always be there to run the company and keep it afloat. During some of those years my brother also helped out here and there, so I could disappear into binge world and the business would remain intact.

But with Dad gone and my brother dealing with his own personal issues, I no longer had that cushion. It was all on me. If I wanted to keep the family income stream going and the company's future bright, I had a lot of work to do. My mission was to keep our employees happy and our customers satisfied. This became my purpose, my reason for living clean every day.

Bottom line: one of us needed to step back and let the other step up, and I ended up being the one to step down. With that one move, everything shifted for the worse in my life once again. It wasn't long before there was unhappiness in my new marriage, because I felt as if there was nothing left to stay sober for without the business. My triggers are not an excuse at all, and my father is not to blame, but I made the decision to go back to the only other thing I knew that could fill the void in my life: cocaine.

CHAPTER 15

PARTYING LIKE A ROCK STAR

Once my father had effectively taken charge again, he and I continued to have arguments about the direction the company should take. On top of that, my brand-new marriage was crumbling. Just as Sandra had noticed the difference in my behavior once I started getting high again, Harvest did, too, and she didn't like it. I could see that I had gotten married with high hopes that our relationship could help stabilize me and keep me from doing drugs. But no relationship can do that. The pattern just repeated itself. Arguments and more arguments.

As soon as my father was running the show, I lost interest in the company. I also realized that I probably rushed into marriage. There was nothing wrong with Harvest: I just think I got married for the wrong reasons and didn't give our relationship time to grow, which led to problems in my home life.

Tired of all the conflict and stress both at home and at work, I wanted an escape, as every addict does. I turned back to what was familiar to me—using. Once again, as I had done countless times in the past, I constructed a system of lies and justifications to convince myself that using just *one* time wouldn't hurt. I also told myself that my father and my wife were the reasons for my drug use. Total delusion.

I chose to deal with the pressure the same way I dealt with it during my marriage to Sandra: I took off on a three-month binge, once again leaving a pregnant wife behind.

I got into my 2003 Porsche 911 and hit the road—alone this time—intending to party in Reno, do some gambling, and have some "fun." As usual, before I traveled, I stopped by my dealer's house and stocked up on cocaine. It was nighttime, and I remember racing up the road toward Sacramento, where I would turn east and head toward Reno. Naturally, I was high and driving way too fast. My binge had technically started a few days earlier, so I was already both tired and wired.

I finally pulled over and got a hotel room in Sacramento, falling back into my old patterns with ease. I figured I would rest, do more drugs, or indulge in a little of both, staying in my room for the night. I didn't want to deal with driving because of the risk of getting arrested, which would end my binge, mess up my high, and get me sent back to jail.

But being alone in a hotel room was lonely and boring. I didn't want to do drugs alone, but I still didn't want to drive anywhere. There had to be an alternative.

I'll call a limo, I thought. *I can take it to Reno, and there will be plenty of time to relax and do drugs on the way. I can have a driver take me around the city without having to worry about getting busted for being under the influence.* So I made a phone call.

A short time later, a stretch limo showed up outside. I left my car in the hotel parking lot and got in.

"I'm Marty," the driver said, introducing himself. "Where do you want to go?"

"Get me to a hotel in downtown Reno," I said.

"Sure thing," he said, and we took off.

I did drugs along the way, and when we arrived, I told Marty which hotel to take me to. After checking in, I went about figuring out where to have a good time. Reno was one of my frequent party towns when I was using. No one knew me, but there were people I could connect with there, especially if I was supplying the drugs.

It was easy for me to recognize any prospective "friends." Even though I had been off cocaine for five years, I could spot the users, the dealers, and the partyers who wanted what I wanted. When you're not doing drugs, and you're not in that world, you don't see the drug culture right under your nose. But when you're looking for it, you pay attention, and you're tuned in. Just as I did when I stopped in Oklahoma City, I found everything I was looking for.

Marty took me wherever I needed to go. He didn't do drugs himself, but he was starting to understand me and the things I liked and wanted to do. So he drove me to places where I could get into the action.

One night I was with a couple of friends, and Marty drove us to a bar that seemed like it was in the middle of nowhere. Inside, rap music thumped loudly and enhanced my party mood.

The place looked perfect. There were two bars and a DJ in the corner. But it seemed like we were the only customers there.

"Give me a bottle of Blue Label," I told the bartender. (Johnnie Walker Blue Label was my drink of choice whenever I hit the clubs.)

"What do you think this is—Vegas?" he asked, laughing. He handed me a bottle of Jack or Crown Royal—I don't remember which.

I walked over to the DJ and got behind his equipment, checked it out, and started talking with him, getting more into the music and the party mood.

By then, there were a few people on the dance floor, but it seemed like even they were all employees. I couldn't spot any other customers.

With a bottle in my hand, I got out on the dance floor and danced a little bit with the ladies who were there.

The next thing I knew, I was being carried out by a couple of bouncers.

"What are you doing?"

"You gotta get out of here," they told me.

"What did I do?"

"You're causing trouble."

"What kind of trouble? What about my friends?"

"What friends?" one bouncer said. "You came in alone."

"What are you talking about? I came in with two friends, and you know it!"

They took me to Marty, who was still waiting.

"What's going on?" I asked him.

"I don't know," he said. "I just saw them escorting you out."

"What about the people I came with?"

"They left a while ago with someone else," he told me.

I was confused, but I checked my pockets and found that my wallet and cash were still there.

"Screw it," I told him. "Take me somewhere else."

He did, and I found another place to party for the night, but without those friends.

Later that night, or maybe early the next morning, I made it back to my hotel room. The people I had gone to the bar with showed up a little while later.

"Where did you go?" I asked them.

They gave me some lame excuse. I still don't know what happened. Do I think someone slipped me a Mickey? Probably. But I have no idea why. Maybe they took some of my cash but not all of it. I have no clue. Complete blackout!

Another time, Marty took me to a different bar outside of town. That night, I had drugs stashed all over his car but didn't take them with me. I just went inside to have a drink and see if I could find someone to party with. Let me tell you, addiction can be a lonely experience, except for the times when you connect with other addicts. Then it begins to feel like what some people might call a family.

The bar was pretty empty, and as I sat there having my drink, looking for some action, the front door opened, and a cop came in with a drug-sniffing dog on a leash.

I panicked. *Is he here for me? Does he know I have drugs? What's happening outside with my driver? Did my driver snitch on me?*

Before the cop had a chance to approach me, I took off through the kitchen, running out the back door as employees stared at me. There was a fence around the place, topped with barbed wire, and in my panicked state, I climbed it, making my way over the top. I cut myself in a couple of places and was bleeding, but I didn't care. Adrenaline was fueling my escape.

I came upon a high hill on the other side of the fence, and I climbed to the top of it, hoping I would be able to see what was going on. The limo and the cop car were the only vehicles in the parking lot, and outside the bar it seemed quiet.

Man, I am screwed, I thought. *If the cop searches the car, I'm going to jail for a long time.*

Even though I had no idea whether the cop would search the car, I didn't want to stick around to find out. I also didn't want to be walking around on the hill, where the cops could spot me. So I lay down on my back, tall grass and weeds surrounding me. It was a clear night, and I looked up at the stars, thinking to myself, as I had so many times before, *What the hell am I doing?* This is the insanity of addiction, and I was living it.

I eventually decided to get up and start walking, not back to the limo but back into town. I started down the other side of the hill, making my way through the desert toward the main road. It was a desolate night with no cars anywhere. There I was, just walking along that road at 3:00 a.m. Next thing I knew, Marty pulled up beside me in the limo.

"Get in," he said. "What the hell are you doing?'

"Didn't you see that cop?" I asked him.

"Yeah. He checked the place out and left. Why'd you take off?"

"I thought he might be looking for me," I said.

"Well, he wasn't looking for you, and he's gone now," Marty said.

I got in the limo, then we drove back to town.

That episode is a good example of how unmanageable my life had become. I was on the run, living a life I was ashamed of, with the need to constantly look over my shoulder. I was always on the alert for law enforcement officers who might have good reason to detain or arrest me. After all, I had a history of drug use, an arrest record, and that limo was loaded with drugs. You might say I had very good reason to be paranoid. That's one of the things I hated most about doing drugs.

Paranoia is a common symptom in anyone who's on cocaine, and it turns out there's a scientific reason for it. Cocaine addicts frequently experience what's called *substance-induced psychosis*, a temporary state of insanity that can occur after using drugs just *one time*. The more you use, the higher the risk of auditory hallucinations, restlessness, and paranoia. Impulsive, dangerous behaviors—which may involve violence, promiscuous sexual activity, and temporary paranoid delusional states—are common. These behaviors can go on for years, even requiring admission to a mental hospital.

I was right on the edge of it all. Sometimes I was okay and could use drugs heavily for days, even going without sleep, and I would not feel paranoid at all. But other times, the insanity would kick in, and I would become extremely agitated. Suddenly I was worried about all kinds of bad things happening, most of which were in my mind. I would stop wanting to engage with people. I wouldn't want to drive around and experience new things. Instead I just wanted to hide. Even partying with other people was no longer fun as I spiraled further down into the abyss of using drugs alone. All the things that had made the drug lifestyle exciting for me seemed to turn against me. Excessive use of coke had turned me into a paranoid loner.

In this state, I was always convinced that someone was after me. Sometimes I drove around with guns in my car, often checking into a hotel to hide from my supposed attackers. Once I got in a room, I'd spread my guns out on the bed, all locked and loaded and all pointing at the door. If anyone—even a maid or a member of the hotel staff—had come through that door, I might have shot him or her. Until my mind settled down, which could take many hours, you could not have convinced me that there was no threat. I was on the edge of total self-destruction, a danger to myself and others.

That's the way it went. Marty and I stayed in Reno for a week.

Just as I did on previous trips, when I started running low on drugs, I hustled some around town, but there was a problem. The quality was never as good as it was when I bought from my own dealers, who knew that I would pay a premium price for better stuff. Local dealers saw me as just another strung-out customer who would take anything they sold me. Although I tried a few different dealers in Reno, none of them was up to my standards. I was stuck and had to settle for using the drugs I could get, which acted as a Band-Aid until I could get more from my regular sources.

"Hey, why don't you take me back to my car in Sacramento?" I finally asked Marty. "I think I'm done here."

He agreed, and we headed back to the hotel where I'd left my car the week before.

I didn't know where I would go next, but I wasn't ready to go home. I had completely abandoned my wife, family, and business. I decided the party was not over just yet.

"Hey, bud, I'm not done partying yet," I told Marty. "I have an idea. Let's go to Vegas."

"Are you serious?" he asked.

"Yeah. I'll pay your expenses and cover whatever you need. I just need to make a stop, and then we can go."

"Okay," he said. "Let me call my boss and make sure it's okay with him."

He called his boss and told him I wanted to go to Vegas in the car and that I would pay his expenses plus the normal rental fee. His boss said yes.

To be clear, Marty never did drugs with me, and he had no drug-related connections in Las Vegas. He was functioning as a driver only, but he would obviously take me wherever I wanted to go.

While we drove toward Vegas, I asked him to stop at the home of one of my regular dealers, where I picked up half a pound of coke, which I figured would last me a decent amount of time.

Then, when we got to Vegas, I found new people to party with. Time flew by, and after what was probably a couple of weeks, Marty approached me.

"Hey, Carlos," he said. "I'm kind of like your personal driver at this point, right?"

"Yeah. And I appreciate it."

"I have some extra uniforms, but it would be nice if I didn't have to go around dressed like this all the time," he said, indicating his clothes. "I know you said you'd pay for my expenses, but could that include cash for some clothes?"

"Sure. Of course."

He went to get something different to wear, and for the next six weeks, he was my personal driver. During the day he'd wait in the car or hang out nearby while I ran errands and did whatever I needed to do. At night, while I was in the clubs, or if I was partying with people in my room, he'd wait until I needed him for something. It was like having a personal valet.

In Vegas, I wanted to stay at nice hotels, but they weren't the kind of places where you can stay for weeks at a time snorting cocaine and smoking rock without raising suspicions. Instead, I bounced around to different places, renting suites for short periods so I looked more like a regular tourist. In a hotel, I liked room service and all the other perks, but I didn't want anyone to figure out what I was doing. Besides, I got bored with the same room day after day. At first, a new hotel would be something different and exciting, but each one would quickly lose its thrill. I bounced my way all down the Strip and even to the hotels surrounding it.

Finding people to party with was a top priority. I was constantly looking for action, not considering what effect that might have on anything back home. As I think about it now, this Vegas binge may have been part of my unconscious exit strategy, my solution to escaping my life and what it had become.

Marty and I would often roll up and down the Strip, Bone Thugs-N-Harmony thumping on the stereo, the windows down. I could hear the sounds of people talking and laughing as they walked the neon-lit streets, and I could hear music coming from the clubs. I would occasionally pick up some party people and have them join me in the limo. In a cocaine-induced euphoria, I was free of responsibility and able to do whatever I wanted. Some might say I was partying like a rock star!

I followed no sleep patterns. I just partied, then crashed, without a real schedule. Before I went into a nightclub, I would smoke a pipe or do a big line in the limo. My inhibitions were down, and I was ready to party like crazy. I wasn't worried about anything. There was no stress. I was living life to the fullest, or so it seemed at the time. Then I would go into a club that had bottle service, buy a bottle of Blue Label, and start off by drinking it out of a glass. But by the end of the night I would be on the dance floor with some woman I met, drinking straight from the bottle. So, of course, whenever I was at these clubs, I would buy drinks for whomever I wanted to party with.

I wasn't aware that all this addictive self-indulgence was actually quite sad. This was no way to live. At the time I thought of this lifestyle as glamorous—though not always. Sometimes I would pass out for long periods of time, while some nights I wanted to stay in my room rather than go out. Was it because I was tired? Or could it have been the paranoia that seemed to come and go? I really had nobody to talk to except Marty. I told him all about my family, my past, and the partying I had done, and we bonded as friends. One night, when I shared with him a desperate moment of my addiction history, I recall that he ended up crying, really feeling my pain. He became a good friend when I needed it. But after around six weeks of taking care of me and finding out who I was, he started to get seriously concerned.

"Carlos," he would tell me. "Maybe you should just go back home and get your life together."

He saw past the rock-star front and into the sad truth of my life. He knew this way of living wasn't normal and that I obviously had a major drug problem. Yes, people go to Vegas to party for a weekend or even a week. But not for weeks on end without any connection to life back at home.

"You need to go home," he pleaded. "I need to go home, too. I can't do this anymore."

"I'm not ready," I told him.

"Well, I am," he stated emphatically. "This is *your* lifestyle, not mine. Come back with me. I'll get you home, I promise."

"No, thanks," I told him. "I'm good."

I was destroying my life, hurting people back home, and I

should have gone with him. But I didn't want the binge to end.

To his credit, he left anyway, stranding me in Vegas. Now I had no driver, and the drugs were running out again.

To keep the "party" going, I found several new local drivers who knew where the drugs, parties, and women were. One of the drivers I found was also a bouncer, and he would get me into any club I wanted. We would walk right in, past the crowd, never waiting in line. I felt like a rock star once again, and I had the best of everything once I was inside.

One night, I remember walking into a club, picking up a table over my head, and moving it to the spot where I wanted it to be. I felt like I owned the place. Clearly, all my inhibitions were down. The combination of cocaine and alcohol can be a dangerous one, even causing a stroke or heart attack because of the elevation of blood pressure. But I didn't know this at the time—or didn't care. Frankly, when I was high, I wasn't afraid of anything. I felt as if I were on top of the world and didn't have to answer to anyone. This sense of deluded entitlement is typical of an addict. I felt as if this was an ideal life . . . except, of course, for the times when I had blackouts and couldn't remember any of it.

One of those times, I vaguely remember being on the dance floor with a bottle of Blue Label in my hand. I started dancing with a girl who was with another guy, but I didn't care about him or what he thought. After I danced with her, I moved from one woman to another, dancing with whomever I wanted. That's the last thing I remember. The next thing I knew, I woke up in my hotel room. My wallet was gone, and I had no idea where it was. I called the driver who'd been with me.

"What happened?"

"Carlos, you ended up fighting with some bouncers at the second club. They grabbed you and threw you out. I picked you up and brought you back to your hotel."

"Where's my wallet?" I asked.

"You threw it at them, and they kept it," he told me. "We can go and try to get it back." (I ended up calling the club and asking, but they had no wallet. A few days later, thanks to my driver, the wallet showed up.)

I don't know if that was the whole truth. I just remember one moment being on the dance floor and waking up in my hotel room the next. There were no foggy interludes, nothing in between. Just a piece of time that disappeared. Once again, did someone put a Mickey in my drink? I'll never know. I was in a complete blackout. That night was just another example of what my life had become—a series of binges, hangovers, and unmanageable moments.

After I hung out with the men who were my new drivers for a while, they knew I was cool, and they trusted me. They invited me to their personal hangouts away from the Strip, where they would drink with their own friends. I had found another little "family" to distract me from reality. Lonely as I was, I liked being part of it. Many of my drivers were Romanian, and their friends were not big fans of Americans. But because I'm Brazilian, they accepted me as one of their own. We became party friends who trusted one another, and we did normal things together, like shooting pool and even bowling.

Then my cash started running out. When I tried to get more, I discovered that my bank accounts were completely drained. I was broke. Meanwhile, my credit cards were canceled for lack of payment. Just two and a half months earlier, I'd started off the trip with plenty of money. But the limos, the clubs, the alcohol, the drugs, and the gambling all added up really fast. What little cash I had in my pocket (and the dwindling supply of cocaine) was not going to last more than a couple of days. I had to replenish my resources, though getting more money would not be easy.

I hired a limousine driver who didn't know me.

"I need you to take me to Sacramento and back," I told him.

"Okay," he said, then gave me a price.

"Sounds good," I told him, and we headed back to Sacramento, where I'd left my car ten weeks earlier. He followed me when I took it to the local Porsche dealer, and for the second time, I sold a car for cash so I could keep the party going.

Then we headed right back to Vegas, and I stayed there until the money from the car sale ran out. Despite the haze I was in, I recall talking to my nine-year-old daughter, Elaina, on the phone. When she asked where I was and when I was coming home, it broke my heart. I don't remember my answer, but it made me feel like a piece of shit. I also called Harvest, who told me that she planned to name our baby Morgan and that she didn't care to have my input into the decision. I didn't blame her.

I was sober enough to realize that it was time to make a major change if I ever wanted to see my children again. I had to stop this downward spiral.

I checked out of the hotel and asked one of my drivers if I could crash at his place while I planned my trip home.

"I ruined my marriage before it even got started," I told him with remorse. "I have a kid I barely know and another one on the way. I can't bear to face my family, but I have to suffer the consequences."

I had just enough money to buy myself a plane ticket home. I flew back to California in January of 2006 and checked myself into Narconon one more time, intending to stay clean for good. Even though I was committed to making amends, there were some things I had broken that could never be repaired.

CHAPTER 16

ANGEL ON MY SHOULDER

During my time in Narconon, I quickly realized that I was fully responsible for the failure of my marriage to Harvest, who had nothing to do with my escape to Vegas. Nor was my father to blame for my binge. Our disagreements about the business were not responsible for my behavior. The decision I made to escape was solely my addictive response to the normal stressors of life. I can't blame anyone for that except myself.

As time passed, I could see how I used the stress in my marriage and conflict at work as excuses to rationalize my return to drugs. Of course, I could have responded differently to these triggers. I could have chosen other ways to deal with the problems in my life. But I didn't.

By this point, Harvest had seen me in full-blown addiction mode, and it had frightened her. She had wanted our marriage to work and had tried to help in any way she could, urging me to go to counseling or enroll in a community service program. That would have involved picking up highway trash or working in soup kitchens for the homeless. I'm sure it was a good program for giving back to society, but I couldn't do it. I wouldn't agree to any of it.

Just as I had in the past, I responded really well to the Narconon model, which is all about creating a drug-free life. I knew that I had to work on making serious internal changes to the way I responded to stressful events. For so many years, I had been on an emotional roller coaster, and it was time to create stability.

While I truly wanted to get clean and was doing well, I didn't have much hope for saving my marriage. Harvest was eight months pregnant when I got back from the Vegas binge, and I was scheduled to still be in rehab when our daughter, Morgan, was born. Thankfully, Narconon allowed me to leave just for that day.

Harvest didn't want me in the delivery room, so I nervously waited outside. Then the magic moment came when I was able to go in and see Morgan. When I held her for the first time, I started crying, overwhelmed with feelings of love and guilt. This was both a joyful moment and a sorrowful one, too, for I realized how much I had given up for my addiction. My marriage was totally over, that much was clear. Harvest had plans to move to a town four hours away, so I knew I would be absent from Morgan's life, just as I'd been absent from Elaina's.

What came next would be some of the hardest months of my life. But the good news was that there was something new going on inside me, a battle for my very soul.

I don't know if you believe in God, but if you do, then you have to believe in the devil. There's no way you can believe in good and not believe that evil exists. I mention this because some of the things you're going to read in the next few chapters talk about my struggles with good and evil. When 2006 came around, I felt like God and the devil were battling for my soul. God, of course, was trying to save it, and devil was trying to damn it forever by pulling me deeper into drugs.

I was clean after my stint at Narconon, abstinent from drugs, but I was about to have a relapse. I could just feel it. At that point, because I needed a safe place to stay for a few weeks, my friend Joe offered to let me stay at his home. But one morning, I impulsively told him, "Joe, I have one last binge to go on." I left his house and headed out . . . straight out to the Catholic church I belonged to, where I prayed.

"God, I am about to slip again and go on a binge," I said. "I need you to watch over me and bring me home safe."

When I look back on it, it seems like such an odd prayer, but I meant every word of it. This was the first time that I ever planned a binge with a clear mind and made the effort to get things right before disappearing in the dark world of addiction.

I left the church and deliberately went to buy drugs, knowing I was heading toward that binge. I was still searching for something, trying to find answers, and I wasn't sure which side I would ultimately give in to—good or evil, life or death. I felt this final escapade was something that would help me decide.

I knew I had messed up my life. I knew people had no reason to trust me. I didn't know how to rebuild that trust and get back to work at A. V. Thomas, much less how to heal the relationships I'd destroyed. It all seemed so overwhelming and exhausting. I even wondered if I could trust myself. Whatever the case, I headed out and bought cocaine, then off I went again.

My plan was to drive two hours west of home to Santa Cruz, California, a place I thought might have been a central battleground between good and evil. A couple of weeks previously, I had been to a Christian church, in my hometown of Atwater, where the people were so friendly and welcoming that, at some point, I started to cry as they surrounded me with love, praying over me. It was beautiful. Afterward, the minister invited me to lunch, and he told me a long story about the curse of Santa Cruz. I don't remember the entire story, but he made a point to tell me all about it, because he understood my struggle with addiction.

As odd as it sounds, this was a very spiritual time in my drug use. What I was experiencing was beyond the high and beyond the party. I felt like I was trying to knock down doors, trying to get to the other side of something that was holding me back from being the person I was meant to be. In my mind, there was evil all around me, constantly obstructing me while I was desperately searching for happiness and peace. Up to that point, it had been a losing battle.

In that frame of mind, I stocked up on drugs and headed for Santa Cruz, looking for who knows what. I do recall a phone call I made on the way. I stopped in the town of Gustine and used a pay phone to call my best friend Brian. I remember sharing with him that this was a battle I was going through, telling him that I was on one last binge. By this point in our friendship, Brian was tired of my explanations and didn't want to hear my crazy excuses for using drugs again. I don't remember his exact words, but he pretty much told me he was "done" with me. Then he hung up.

I got back in the car and continued on my journey to Santa Cruz, not knowing what the hell I was planning on doing next. I even pulled into a Narconon office in Santa Cruz when I first got there and signed myself in, but then left after only a few minutes while I was waiting to see a counselor. Talk about conflicted.

I only stayed in Santa Cruz for around three days, hanging out and looking for answers as I tried to figure out what I was going through. I finally headed back toward home, eventually finding new party friends, some of the worst people you can imagine. I met a fellow addict named Rachel, who I knew was bad news. But I kept partying with her and her friends anyway. I realized that these were not the kinds of people I should be hanging out with. But as you know by now, I liked the risk and danger of being around fellow partiers. It's truly scary to say this, but I was at the point in my life where I honestly didn't care what happened to me. I knew this was evil at work. It was like the old cartoons in which an angel sits on one shoulder and the devil sits on the other, whispering conflicting messages into some poor guy's ears.

One late night I remember being parked in someone's driveway, not knowing what to do with myself. What time was it? Why was I there? I didn't know. The shadowy light around me felt threatening. I felt that whatever was going on, I was not going to survive it. But what difference did it make? Everybody I ever cared about was finished with me. There was nothing left. I had burned every bridge. I had hit rock bottom. Now, on this weird night, I felt like something bad was about to happen. The feeling scared me to death. I called a really close friend, a woman I could trust. I told her I needed her to come pick me up and take me somewhere safe. Her boyfriend asked her not to bring me to their home, so she ended up taking me to the home of another good friend. As she drove, we started talking. To me, she seemed like Jesus Christ or some kind of savior, like an angel who had come down to protect me from whatever might have happened if I had stayed on the course I was on.

But even angelic intervention didn't stop me.

After returning home from this mini binge, I was in a really bad place, mentally and spiritually. I was tired of the chaos and how messed up my life was. Even the simplest things, like getting up to take a shower or making a meal, were exhausting, and I could still feel the presence of darkness all around me.

I felt like my house was a big part of the problem. It had been the scene of so many drug parties, filled with evil people and lingering drug-filled memories. Perhaps even an evil presence was dwelling there. It was frightening and depressing. Because I wanted a fresh start, in my altered state, I decided the best solution was to cleanse the house by burning it down!

Some people say rock bottom is when you're broke, with no place to live, no food to eat, and no friends. I had been there numerous times. I remember one time being really hungry and wanting something to eat. I went to my sister's house thinking she would feed me, but instead she slammed the door in my face. That was the reality I was in.

But that's only one type of rock bottom. It can go far beyond that, to a point where you don't *want* food, shelter, friends, or money. In that state, you're ready for a total reset. You know you need to change your life, and you'll do anything to make it happen.

That's where I was when I decided to burn down my house.

Often when people say things like this, they don't really mean it. In the moment of truth, they might back down, realizing there is always a limit. But I was absolutely serious. Of course, it was an insane idea, the product of a mind that had been cooked on coke. I was impulsive and headstrong, and I believed that the only way to purge the evil out of me was to set the house on fire. I had always been a person who was all in or not in at all. Well, when it came to craving a huge change, I was all in, even if I was misguided.

One late night, I pulled things out of the house that I thought were valuable and didn't want to lose—some jewelry and family photos. Then I went around randomly yanking things off the walls, throwing them around and knocking things over. I was a madman. But I didn't care. Everything I left behind was going to burn anyway. None of it mattered, because I already had nothing. I'd lost all my furniture twice to ex-wives, even down to the blinds on the windows. I'd sold cars that I loved and threw away enormous sums of money. Possessions meant nothing to me. I needed to be stripped down to the bare walls of my being so that I could rebuild. I was desperate for a change. A total reboot.

I thought about what my alibi would be and how I would get away with it. I even thought of my neighbors and how I could make sure the fire wouldn't spread to their homes. I had gas cans all ready, along with three lighters, just in case one of them didn't work. I was a frenzied mess, standing in front of my house, gas cans by my side, lighters in my hand, ready to do the unthinkable.

Then something stopped me. Maybe the angel on my shoulder spoke louder than the devil. Maybe I was concerned about what my parents would think if I did such a thing, or I might have been worried about the safety of the homes around me or the possibility that I would be caught and arrested.

That's when I realized that I was actually thinking clearly. I had, for just one moment, stepped outside the blurry bubble where I usually lived. In the bubble there's no sense of time, no sense of life going on around you. It's an endless expanse of nothingness. Just one long day.

But in that moment of clarity, something clicked, and I found myself in the harsh light of reality. There was no way I could do this. I was able to ask myself what would have happened if I'd followed through and hurt someone. What if I had gotten caught? How would burning down my home really have changed my life?

I'll never know, because a few days later, something entirely different changed everything for me.

CHAPTER 17

THE NIGHT

September 14, 2006: The day had been warm, in the seventies, but by midnight, the temperatures had dropped into the midfifties.

Rap music was thumping throughout my house as my party friends and I mingled and moved between the living room and the yard, all of us feeling the effects of the cocktail of drugs in our bodies.

A pile of cocaine sat on the bar, some of it divided into long, neat lines. I don't know how much there was, but it was a heap, plenty for everyone. Bottles of alcohol were everywhere, and a bag of weed sat on the table, too, which of course didn't interest me as much as the cocaine.

Drug parties were a social thing for me, and I had partied with numerous people, from friends to strangers. The one thing we all had in common was our love of drugs.

It seemed like this particular night would go on forever. When we started smoking cocaine in addition to snorting it, things got even crazier. As always, there was plenty of variety and enough for everyone, so the party would never stop. At one point I remember standing in the living room talking to a guy I'd partied with in the past. But what happened next I will never understand. Remember—coke addicts are frenetic and impulsive, and I was high as a kite.

In my semipsychotic state, fueled by coke, I suddenly felt an overwhelming feeling of evil all around me and an overpowering urge to escape it. It was the most intense paranoia I'd ever experienced.

The evil felt so real that I rushed to my front door, threw it open, and ran as fast as I could down the street to a neighbor's house.

As I reached the doorstep, I pulled my leg back and kicked in the door. It flew open, banging against the wall in the foyer. I was a wild man. A set of stairs led to the second floor. I sat down on the lowest step. Then I sat there with my head in my hands, breathing heavily.

How did I get here? How did I get to this low point in my life?

"What are you *doing* here?" exclaimed a man from the top of the stairs, his voice full of fear and confusion.

"I don't know," I said quietly, without looking up.

"You kicked in our door. How can you not know?"

"I don't know," I said again, confused, looking up to see the silhouette of a man with a woman cowering behind his left shoulder.

I needed to think, to process what I felt and what I did, so I dropped my head into my hands again and sat there. Breaking and entering was a new low, even for me.

"What the hell do you want? You can't be here!" the man shouted.

"I know," I said even more quietly, shaking my head.

Then his voice softened a bit. "What's wrong, young man?" he asked.

"I don't know," I said.

I heard the woman whispering to him.

"I have to call the cops. You know that," the man said.

"I know. Go ahead. I don't care."

"Do you need help?" he asked, the tone of his voice softening again. He sensed that I wasn't in my right mind. I turned to look at him.

"I'll go if you let me use your phone," I answered.

"What for?"

"I need to call my father."

The man bravely made his way down the steps and handed me

a phone. For all he knew I was armed and might have shot him. But once again, I'd encountered yet another good person in the midst of my personal hell.

I dialed the number, not knowing if Dad would answer in the middle of the night, but he did.

"Dad, I need your help."

"My son, my son," he said. "Oh, my son."

"I need your help," I repeated into the phone.

"Oh my son, I'm so sorry."

As he said this, I sat there rubbing my head, listening in silence, trying to make sense of it all. The people near me stood by in silence as well.

Then my father hung up. He wasn't coming.

It wasn't the first time he'd received a call like this. He probably would have helped me if I'd been clean, but he knew I was high. He knew there was nothing he could do to help me. Even if he'd come to pick me up and brought me to his house or to rehab, he knew that in a matter of weeks or months, we'd be right back where we were.

I put the phone down on the steps and walked through the shattered door frame into the night, not looking back or saying a word to the people who lived there.

I reached the middle of the street and started walking, yelling at the top of my lungs, "I love cocaine! I love Elaina! I love Morgan!"

I must have had the need to yell the names of the things I loved most. Why?

Time seemed to slow down. I kept yelling the same thing over and over, wanting the world to hear as I walked the streets of my neighborhood.

"I love cocaine! I love Elaina. I love Morgan!"

It seemed like I had been walking forever when I stopped in the middle of an intersection and sat down. I stared at the asphalt with my head in my hands. A car drove by, and I slowly looked up and offered a small wave.

I wonder now what its occupants thought of me, but at that moment, I didn't care.

I'm not sure how much time passed, but it felt like forever as I sat there. Then something spurred me to get up.

I started walking again, and as soon as I was on the move, I began to yell once more.

"I love cocaine! I love Elaina. I love Morgan!"

Over and over, I shouted these words into the night. Perhaps I was trying to satisfy both God and the devil somehow. I have no idea.

Then I paused. Something came over me, and I started running, this time to another house, where I started kicking that door, trying to get in. I kicked it repeatedly as hard as I could, but it didn't move. I felt the jolt of every kick through the joints in my leg all the way up to my hip. The door was solid, so I took a step back and tried again. Then I took two steps back and tried again.

An angry voice came from the other side.

"I'm a cop. I have a gun pointed at you through the door. If you don't stop, I will shoot."

The voice was calm, businesslike. Professional. Definitely sounded like a cop.

Still I kept kicking the door. I didn't care if he shot me. I had to escape the nightmare my life had become, and all I knew was that there was a door in the way, and I had to get to the other side.

"I'm a cop, and I *will* shoot!"

The next thing I knew I was back on the road, walking and shouting again. I must have realized that I wasn't going to knock *that* door down, so I continued on my rampage.

I eventually ended up in someone's backyard and up on a

balcony overlooking the countryside. It felt as if I were in the middle of nowhere, and I could see forever. The air was calm, without even a breeze. No dogs barked.

I started shouting my mantra again to break that silence. I cupped my hands to amplify my voice.

"I love cocaine!"

"I love Elaina!"

"I love Morgan!"

I yelled those words over and over, pausing occasionally.

Where am I?

How many miles am I from my house?

How did I get here?

I didn't think of it then, but now I can just picture the family who lived there peeking through the curtains, wondering who I was and what I was doing. Can you imagine what you would have thought?

"I love cocaine!"

"I love Elaina!"

"I love Morgan!"

I wanted my voice to carry as far as I could see, to the horizon and beyond.

At some point I started running through backyards, jumping the fences between them. I remember getting clotheslined by something and falling. Then I got up and kept running.

I ended up back on the main road, walking down the center line. I started to recognize the homes around me. Shadows from the trees broke up the gray of the pavement. I'd come around the block, full circle. I rounded the corner looking toward my own house once again.

There were cop cars everywhere. Blue and red lit up the night, and spotlights were aimed at my house. No one was looking my way.

I could have escaped. I could have thrown away the drugs in my pocket, and the cops never would have found them. I could have turned and walked away into the night. But for some reason, I walked straight toward them. It all needed to end.

Finally some officers spotted me, but nothing happened. They didn't approach me or chase me. I continued walking toward them while they stared at me. When I got close enough, I dropped down to my knees, then onto my face. They didn't say a word, and I didn't say anything, either. I turned my head to the side, eyes wide open, my cheek against the asphalt, and put my hands behind my back, preparing to be cuffed.

I remember one officer saying, "Man, this guy is fifty-one fifty."

I didn't know what he meant at the time.

I felt them pull me to my feet. They asked if I had anything in my pockets, and I felt hands search me. The officer pulled some cocaine out of my front pocket.

They arrested me for possession of a controlled substance, disorderly conduct, and being under the influence of drugs. Even though the officer had referred to it, they *didn't* hold me under section 5150 of the California Welfare and Institutions Code, which, I later learned, allows authorities to detain someone up to seventy-two hours if that person is perceived to be a danger to himself or to others.

The cops drove me to the county jail. While they were booking me, I lay back on a bench. I needed to be still, to disconnect, so I wasn't going to move.

"Get up!" one of them said. "Come on. We need to get you to your cell."

I wouldn't move and didn't say a word.

"Stand up. Come on. We need you to walk with us, now!"

I still didn't respond. I closed my eyes and focused on nothing. No one.

"Help me out here," the man called to nearby officers, then I felt strong hands lifting me up into the air. I cracked my eyes open just enough to see that there were four of them carrying me.

In my distorted perception, it felt like they transported me a very long way. Then I felt myself airborne before I struck the hard floor. I lay there, not moving.

I heard the cell door slam closed. I shut my eyes and knew this horrible night had finally come to an end. Then I passed out.

CHAPTER 18

RACING AND THE BIRTH OF 51FIFTY

They only kept me in jail for one night. Fortunately, the guy whose door I kicked in didn't press charges, and he didn't even ask to be reimbursed for the cost of repairing the door.

For the first couple of days after getting out of jail, I decided to stay home and sleep it off. I finally woke up feeling physically better and sensing that something was different. Usually when I came off a binge, I didn't eat well or get enough rest. But this time I did. I took care of myself until I was ready to decide what I was going to do with my life.

Then, the first time I went out, I got into my truck, turned the key, and on came the song "Knockin' Doorz Down" by Pimp C.

It was the first time I had ever heard that song. I sat there listening, thinking that's exactly what I had done a couple of nights before! I had knocked down my neighbor's door, insane as it was, and I had to ask myself why. It felt like that song had come on for a reason, so I sat there for a minute, deep in thought.

Music had always been a big part of my party life, and whatever tune was playing affected my mood. I had always kept my collection of CDs in the car so I could play the album that best fit the state of mind I wanted to be in. Of course, that set of discs included the music I enjoyed partying to the most. Once in a while I would hear a new song on the radio that would match what was going on with my life.

That morning in my truck, it seemed as if exactly the right song was playing at exactly the right moment. It wasn't because of the lyrics, because honestly, I didn't know them. It was the title of the song itself and the beat that drew me in and made that song significant in the moment.

It took me a little while after I started to get clean to realize what "Knockin' Doorz Down" would mean to me and why it was so important that I'd heard it at a time when I really did start to change my life.

For the thirteen years leading up to The Night, I felt as if I had been locked in a room surrounded by doors, each representing a potential choice I could make. Before The Night, I'd tried certain doors that other people—cops, judges, addiction counselors, and well-meaning friends and family—told me to try. But none of those doors opened onto the path of lifelong change. I now realize that other people couldn't possibly know what would work for me. I knew that *I* needed to find the right door, and I knew that when I did, I would find the best parts of myself waiting on the other side, saying, "Hey, Carlos, what took you so long?!"

After thirteen years as an active addict, I felt as if I had finally walked through the right door, but I had to literally kick it open to break through it.

The first thing I decided after The Night was to abstain from all mind-altering substances for one full year. That meant no drugs, alcohol, or cigarettes. I marked my calendar and made a promise to myself. I knew if I had alcohol in the house, I would be tempted to drink it, so I rounded up all the bottles, including the expensive wines I had collected, and gave them away. If I was going to do this, I needed to do it right. So purging my house was the first step. That meant doing whatever it took.

Yes, I'd made promises like this dozens of times and broken all of them, but something about my resolution this time felt different to me. They always say in twelve-step programs that you reach your bottom when you stop digging. And I was going to stop *now*.

I knew how jittery I would inevitably feel without any drugs to numb my system. I also knew that boredom and lack of purpose were huge triggers for me, bringing about a state of mind that would send me back into an addictive cycle.

So first and foremost, I needed something to occupy my time. I needed to stay busy—extremely busy. At first I tried going back to college and taking some business classes. Then, for the first time in years, I picked up the trumpet, the instrument I had played throughout my school years. At the same time, I took a water polo class at college.

Well, it was great that I tried all this. But college only worked for one semester or so, because I felt foolish enrolling in a beginning business class when I was already operating a successful multi-million-dollar enterprise of my own. Water polo didn't suit me, either, because my classmates were mostly members of the water polo team—all of them younger and more experienced. I felt like the old man on the team. The trumpet, while fun, wasn't that exciting.

Still, college carried me through the first months of my total sobriety and drug-free life, and it was the first time I had been completely clean since 1990.

During this period, I knew I was finally serious when I avoided social situations that involved alcohol or smoking. For example, if I went to a birthday party or a wedding, I would make an appearance, then leave quickly. I didn't want to put myself in a situation in which everyone was drunk and partying, even though I would be there with family and close friends, because I knew I would be tempted to join in.

So essentially, I stayed away from any person or situation that would trigger me to go back to smoking or drinking. Even though cigarettes and alcohol were not my primary issues and didn't cause my cocaine addiction, I wanted to be completely free of all mind-altering substances.

It was at this point in my life that I started a new relationship that turned out to be long-lasting. I wasn't thinking about finding love again, nor did I feel like I needed a woman to help keep me clean. Marriage was the furthest thing from my mind.

But in 2006, just a few months before The Night, I met a woman who would help me change my life without even knowing it. This was during a relatively clean period when I had traveled to British Columbia, Canada, to play in a golf tournament with some corporate clients.

Soon after I arrived in BC, a group of us went out to dinner. A beautiful woman named Aysia—a sweet, soft-spoken, very petite blonde with a great sense of humor, a buyer for one of the produce companies we worked with—was invited along.

Fortunately, I sat next to her at dinner, and we hit it off right away. There was an instant attraction. She was so easy to talk to. We had a lot in common. We talked quite a bit about our work in the produce world and her love for organic foods and my passion about growing organic sweet potatoes. Even though I was eleven years older and quite experienced in the produce world, she knew more about all the different types of vegetables than I did—including sweet potatoes. She was totally a foodie. We hung out late that night, talking and dancing, really connecting.

But then I went on a binge and stopped calling her until I eventually got clean. I remember her trying to get hold of me by phone, but I wasn't calling her back. I had started to spiral down yet again into my usual pattern of using and disappearing.

Thankfully, she gave me another chance, and the next time we saw each other, The Night had come and gone, and I was clean and sober.

I remember we went to a restaurant during her first visit to California. I told her I had something important to tell her. "I'm not drinking, and I've decided to stop it for one year." She didn't dig for more information. She said, "Okay," and we moved on to another subject. (I later found out she was just relieved that I didn't tell her I was married!)

As our relationship developed, I discovered wonderful traits in Aysia. She was the most uncomplicated, down-to-earth woman I had ever dated. Her simple, honest way of loving me introduced me to a new part of myself. Aysia and I ended up getting married on April 23, 2011, in the town of Napa, California. It was a small wedding, and only our closest family and friends were invited.

Aysia let me be me and let me do what I needed to do to get myself on the right track. Up until I met her, I had never been in a relationship where I was completely sober the entire time, every day. When my mind was clean and clear, I learned how to handle pressure and conflict in all parts of my life in a responsible way. Instead of running off on a binge to escape it all, I was able to stay in a conversation, talk through problems, and work cooperatively for solutions. Narconon taught me the basics, things I knew before but lost during my thirteen years of addiction. Aysia was there to do and be exactly what I needed—someone to love me, support me, and, most important, believe in me.

———

The more I thought about how I was going to stay off drugs, the more I realized I was going to need something exciting to keep me out of trouble. It would have to start with a genuine passion, something I truly loved.

I grew up dreaming about being a race car driver. In fact, I was crazy about fast cars as a kid and had posters all over my bedroom of Lamborghinis, Ferraris, Vectors, Porsches—all my dream cars. I knew even as a little boy that I wanted to own my own car as soon as I could. That's why I diligently saved all the money I earned at A. V. Thomas.

When I bought my 1971 Porsche 911, at the age of sixteen, I didn't even know how to drive a stick shift, so I had the manager at A. V. Thomas test-drive it for me. Afterward, he and some other guys taught me how to drive it. Like the cart before the horse, it was the car before the license!

I admit that I was a maniac in that car. I loved to go fast. I would race people off stop signs, do 360s in parking lots or in the middle of streets, barrel around corners, and drive at twice the speed limit whenever I could get away with it. If a sign told me it was safe to take a corner at thirty miles per hour, I did it at sixty; if it said fifty miles per hour, I wanted to do it at a hundred. At heart, I was a street racer; I had never driven on a racetrack before. I knew that given the chance to do so, I would love the excitement of it. Ever since childhood, I imagined myself driving a race car in competition, with cheering fans in the stands.

I grew up knowing nothing about the racing world. In fact, as an adult, I knew nothing about racing competitively. I didn't know anybody who raced. I never went to any races, nor did I know where any racetracks were located. I didn't even watch racing on TV. Though I might have pursued racing earlier in my life, I never did because it didn't seem feasible: I was consumed with going to school, playing sports, and working at the family business. Later, as an adult, I was either working or bingeing on cocaine. That racing dream in the back of my mind never seemed real. I never thought it could actually happen.

When I managed to become sober and drug-free, I knew that to stay clean forever, I needed to do something completely different from anything I had ever done before. In short, now was the time to chase my dream. So, in January of 2007, a few months after The Night, I walked into a store called David's Racing Products and asked the owner, Mike David, how to get started in racing.

"What kind of racing do you want to do?" he asked.

"NASCAR-type racing," I told him. "Where are there some tracks around here?"

He mentioned the Madera Speedway, a third-of-a-mile track where speeds could get up to a hundred miles per hour on the straightaway. He also told me about someone looking to sell what's called a late model. Without any hesitation, I went and bought it. This type of car is custom-built from front to back. The body of the car might look like a recognizable brand-name sports car on the outside, but it belongs to a different species. It may have four wheels, an engine, and a drivetrain, but that's pretty much where the similarities end.

Race cars are custom-engineered to put out lots of horsepower in order to plow through the straightaways and navigate fast around corners at the track. Yes, horsepower is important. But that power needs to be calculated, ensuring that the tires get a good grip on the racing surface and that the vehicle handles smoothly around the corners in order to keep it from losing traction.

As I quickly learned, racing was not going to be easy. A late model isn't just a car with a steering wheel and a gas pedal. I would have to learn the technical side of racing, which I knew nothing about. Even though I didn't yet know anyone in the racing world, that was not going to stop me.

I took the car home, called the track, and found out when practice days were. Then I called my best friends, Brian and Joe, and told them I wanted to get into racing. I asked if they wanted to learn about it and be my crew. They both agreed right away. Joe was an automotive mechanic, which helped a lot.

We threw some tools into a plastic crate, put the car on one of the sweet potato company field trailers, and headed for the track.

I admit that I had no clue how to drive the car. I thought it was just a matter of stepping on the gas and driving as fast as possible. How hard could it be?

I was, of course, dead wrong. Racing is an art, and we were amateurs. We were spinning out left and right, hitting walls. I didn't know that I was driving too fast for that track and way too fast for the car. It was amazing I didn't destroy my race car or injure myself or others. At first, the experienced racers just laughed at us, but eventually they started helping us out and giving us tips, even though they were using racing lingo we didn't understand. They talked about adjusting shocks, springs, and sway bars. They asked us about what tire pressure we were running and what kind of tire stagger we had. We were like, *What?!* We had no idea what we were doing or what we *should* be doing. But our fellow racers were really cool guys who helped us learn the language, and we were grateful for it.

Driving a car around a track is, of course, much more difficult than driving on the street. The main thing I had to learn was how to slow down and be smooth. I learned to understand apex, breaking point, and drive-off. Go gentle on the brake, find that perfect roll speed, keep all the tires flat on the track, and don't overdrive the corners. It feels like you're going slower than you really are, and that's disorienting at first. There's always a fastest way around the track, but without someone showing you what it is, you don't know.

There was so much to learn, and I had to do it fast. I bought the car in January, knowing that the racing season started in March. Along with all the other preparations, we needed to come up with a car number. I thought of using one of my high school sports numbers, maybe 66 or 32, the numbers I'd worn in football and basketball. But they no longer meant much to me. If this was going to be the passion that saved my life, the car number had to mean something.

I also wanted to create a logo that would represent all the positive things that make a person great. I wanted it to be a symbol, a reminder of who I was before drugs and who I was always meant to be. It would become my own personal family crest. It had to represent my journey—where I'd been and where I was going.

I thought back to The Night, the point when everything turned around for me. I kept hearing the cop saying, "This guy is fifty-one fifty." I decided my car would be number 51, and I would design a logo with the number 51 and the word "fifty" spelled out underneath it.

I had the number decaled onto the door and the logo decaled onto the hood of my car, but I never explained the meaning of it to anyone. Most people think it's just a random number. In fact, this is the first time I've shared the true meaning behind the number and the logo to anyone.

At first, people who knew about the 5150 statute came to believe it meant that I was chasing my "crazy" dream of racing cars, which is true. People also said the logo meant that I was crazy to start racing at the age of thirty-five, which is also true. But the real meaning of the logo is that it represents power—power over ourselves and our future. We all have control of who we are and who we want to be. The logo conveys that no substance should have that power over us.

In short, 51FIFTY became a symbol of greatness, one that keeps me focused on doing great things and changing not just myself but also the world. It's a lifestyle. It stands for pushing yourself . . . finding your passion, knowing your dreams, and working hard, always striving to make those dreams a reality. It's all about committing to the hard road, the path that you know is going to be the toughest as well as the most rewarding. Go after it, grab it, make it happen.

The logo helps remind me to make the right choices so I can wake up every day grounded in living healthfully and working hard. It's about believing in yourself and having faith that you can make a difference in this world. We all need to *believe*!

Once I had the number on the car, it was time to race. There were skeptics. But it didn't matter how many people told me that race car driving is dangerous and that I shouldn't take the risk at thirty-five.

In fact, their skepticism only served to strengthen my resolve. I embraced the 51FIFTY logo, which represents a person who never quits, meets all challenges head-on, and doesn't let fear dictate his or her decisions.

I believe that everyone has the opportunity for greatness. Once you decide you don't want to live an ordinary life, and you do something about it, you become one of us. You can't be afraid to stand out from the rest. You only reach the top by tuning out the naysayers and taking a chance.

The first time we finished a race, the car was trashed. There's a photo showing our battered car with no fenders, no bumpers—all bare frame. Yet we were jumping for joy even though we came in last! We were holding pieces of the car up in the air, happy as can be. Why? Because we took the checkered flag and finished the race. To us it meant that we came from nothing and finished what we started.

The entire crew was proud of themselves, having arrived at the track with zero experience, a beaten-up box of tools, and a car carried on an agriculture trailer. We didn't know a thing about racing, but we were totally in the game, though still rough in our skills. I often spun out and wound up at the back of the field. But I wanted it bad. I think I had a reputation for being an aggressive driver, but I didn't care.

Sometimes I'd be racing against cars all around me at high speeds, but I never worried about the dangers of it. I mean, with the lifestyle I had led—all the drugs and dumb things I did—I was just happy to be alive. Of course, I realized the risks on the track—some racers die, and others get seriously injured—but I was following every protocol I could in terms of preparation, and I wasn't going to worry about it.

My father, however, wasn't crazy about my racing. In fact, he hated it. He wanted me to focus all my energy and concentration on the business. He felt as if racing was going to be too distracting. But it never interfered with my work at the company. Maybe Dad didn't fully realize the vital role racing played in keeping me clean. I tried to explain it to him, but he couldn't understand why I needed something besides willpower to keep me from using again. He and my mom had suffered a lot during the time I was on drugs. After I got clean, they were relieved and happy for me but not entirely clear on how important racing was to my state of mind.

When I'm in my race car, I'm completely focused. I don't think about *anything* other than what's directly in front of me. All I do is concentrate on what I need to do in the moment: drive that car and finish that race. Period.

Racing takes intense concentration, and you're constantly thinking about turns, hard and soft braking, smooth acceleration, and cars that are inches away and waiting for you to make a mistake. It's literally a matter of life and death.

Any other thoughts disappear while you're under this kind of pressure. In my case, racing keeps me grounded in the present. It clears my mind.

Sure, the excitement on the track is a big part of the appeal—the danger, the competition, the high speed, the moment-to-moment risks. That edginess satisfies a basic need in me. Drugs had that same adrenaline-boosting effect. But racing is a far better option. Now I can go home at night, sleep in my bed, be with my family, go to work, and experience the best of both worlds. I wake up in the morning, I work out, I'm in the office all day, I have meetings. Dinnertime comes, and I enjoy it with Aysia. Then I go to sleep again. Everything's structured, a much better way of life for sure.

During our first race weekend, in 2007, all the teams were approached by Valley Children's Hospital and asked to participate in a fund-raiser they were planning to hold at the racetrack. The event was called Loose Change, and every team was asked to spend a week collecting change from drawers, pockets, cars, neighbors, and friends. Our crew banded together, and we raised more money than any other team, which earned us the honor of being invited to the hospital to make the donation in person.

It felt incredible to make a real difference in that way, and from that day forward, contributing to charity became part of our mission. We united Carlos Vieira Racing with the brand 51FIFTY to express the idea that life isn't just about believing in yourself and wanting more: it's also about helping others along the way. Once our mission to give back became public, people came together behind our message of self-empowerment and generosity.

The fans at the track liked our logo and the race gear we were wearing—the T-shirts, hats, and such—and they asked if any of it was for sale. And I thought to myself, *Wow—we can sell merchandise with our 51FIFTY logo on it and donate the proceeds to organizations that help families in need!* I reached out to a T-shirt and apparel printing company, and that's how the 51FIFTY product line began.

Aysia, who had no particular background in merchandising or design, agreed to help me launch the 51FIFTY apparel line. She helped me figure out how to start the brand from scratch. From that point forward, we added new products. Today we have an actual brick-and-mortar storefront in Livingston, California, and a whole product line that includes workout gear, water bottles, coffee mugs, watches, beer pitchers, stickers, sunglasses, you name it—even a 51FIFTY onesie for infants. You can't start them too early.

We also created a line of 51FIFTY energy drinks, which contain a blend of maca and astragalus, roots known to increase energy, boost the immune system, strengthen vitality, and aid in resisting fatigue. I was very involved in the creation of the drink, and I even came up with a flavor that included nature's superfood: you guessed it—the sweet potato! I also created the motto found on the can and on our line of apparel, "Live the Madness," or LTM.

What does it mean? The phrase came from my own struggles and the need to live a healthful lifestyle filled with passion and purpose. To live "through" the madness of life is to conquer one's destiny, to put every last bit of your energy and power into your accomplishments. When life is trying to drag you down or hold you back, you overcome those roadblocks and keep moving forward. We all need to rise above the chaos in this world and fulfill our true potential. We need to live the madness!

At one point I also developed 51FIFTY vodka and produced four hundred cases made from my family's own patented variety of sweet potato, the Stokes Purple. The entire inventory was donated to my nonprofit organization, the Carlos Vieira Foundation, which I started in 2007 but became a 501(c)(3) organization in 2009, which just happened to be the year we won our first race. The purpose of the foundation is to raise money for families in need, with all profits from the vodka and other 51FIFTY merchandise funding our efforts.

The concept for the foundation began with the Loose Change fund-raiser but expanded when we hosted a steak dinner that raised $23,500. At first, we didn't have any recipient in mind for the money. Then I thought of an employee at our company named Billie, a single mom whose young son had just been diagnosed with autism. Her struggle really broke my heart, and I wanted to help her.

Billie told me about a place called the Challenged Family Resource Center (CFRC), which helps special-needs families but at that point didn't have a program specifically for autism. I gave the money to CFRC to help them start a small center for families like Billie's. From there I got inspired to create a campaign called the Race for Autism, which holds fund-raisers throughout the year to support the CFRC. Our first year's goal was to raise $51,500, but we exceeded that amount.

After that we realized we had the means to support several organizations, so we divided the money between CFRC, Autism Speaks, and FEAT (Families for Effective Autism Treatment).

We now support a variety of other organizations as well, increasing awareness, hosting community support events and fund-raisers, and awarding grants to families in need through our Direct Help program.

Talk about a complete change of life. Just a couple of years earlier, I was strung out on cocaine, still caught in the madness of it all. But then my personal and professional lives underwent a transformation—the angel won and the devil was defeated.

My racing career and my philanthropic work were both getting off the ground at the same time. I soon created another campaign called the Race 2B Drug Free. We work with local schools to schedule presentations by former drug users who share their stories of addiction and the difficulties of getting clean. We also created an after-school boxing program called Gloves Not Drugs, designed to keep kids off the streets and away from drugs and gangs.

Once the 51FIFTY brand became well known and our products were gaining attention in the marketplace, we received some criticism from mental health advocates who felt that any references to the 5150 section of the California code were offensive to people who suffer from mental illness as well as to people who'd had negative experiences with that particular law.

Also, for the same reason, a controversy erupted over our use of the phrase "Live the Madness" on our clothing and energy-drink can: some people thought those words were offensive to people with mental health issues. I couldn't believe it. It seemed as if those so-called health advocates were twisting an inspirational slogan into something that would be perceived as disrespectful, promoting a stigma about mental illness. For a few weeks, I was on TV and in the newspapers defending us, and there was a rally behind our brand. I thought political correctness had gone too far.

Anybody who knows my story understands that I would

never degrade someone who has a mental illness. After all, I was out of my mind on The Night, which was the catalyst for everything good that happened after it. If it hadn't been for the cops taking me away, I might not have lived through that night. I wouldn't have changed my life, and I wouldn't be doing what I'm doing now.

Long story short: I point-blank refused to change the name of our energy drink or the brand itself. As I explained to our critics, the name represents "a person who never quits, who meets all challenges head-on, doesn't feel fear, pushes the limit, and is determined enough to chase his or her dream." To change the name of the brand would have sent the exact opposite message—the reverse of who I am and what the brand is about.

To address this, I started another campaign called the Race to End the Stigma, not only to change the perception of people who are living with mental illness but also to change the way those who are affected by it perceive themselves. People have to understand that one in five Americans has experienced some form of mental illness and that half of all those illnesses begin by the age of fourteen, which is why we send speakers to schools to discuss mental health awareness and foster early detection.

From my own history, I know the pain of addiction and depression and really feel for anyone who struggles with it. I'm proud that our project donates to organizations that provide needed resources and education for mental health awareness, research, and support.

You might be wondering how all this—race car driving and foundation activism—suddenly worked to keep me sober when nothing else could. After all, multiple rehabs, two failed marriages, neglect of my children, and time in jail . . . none of those realities got me off drugs. What was different this time?

I had found a passion that totally engaged me, something I could do for myself and others. I feel as if race car driving to benefit a greater purpose is a mission that fits me. It's 100 percent *me*, the best of me. 51FIFTY *keeps me focused and keeps me going strong*. It's about taking control of your life rather than giving that control to drugs. I'm not going to ever do that again.

I know deep inside what I should be doing and who I want to be in life. We all make bad decisions, listening to a voice in our heads that persuades us to do something we shouldn't. But 51FIFTY is all about drawing on your willpower, strength, and courage to make the right choice. I'm not just some guy living his dream racing cars but rather somebody who has looked at the darkest part of himself. I'm a guy who allowed drugs to take over my life. But I'm bigger than that. I deserve more than that. That's why I changed my life and figured out what I needed to do to be drug-free.

Nobody *told* me what to do to recover—not the drug counselors, not the cops or the judges, not my wives or my family. Who would have ever believed that a passionate hobby combined with a charitable foundation could result in the best rehab of my life? Now I'm in complete control of how I spend every minute of my day, and I feel connected to my thoughts and feelings rather than wanting to push them away.

I am no longer looking for an escape from life or a release from boredom through drugs. In fact, I'm rarely bored nowadays and always busy. I'm focused on the family business 110 percent and focused on what I can do through my foundation to help others. I sleep and drink business. I'm a businessman to the core. When I go to bed at night, I don't feel regretful or ashamed of what happened during my day. It's a life filled with productivity, love for my wife, children, and family. I also continue to work on expanding the 51FIFTY brand to serve others, including those who are already on the right path, the path they know is true to themselves.

You can say that I follow the "Live the Madness" lifestyle every day. Yes, we live in a crazy world full of madness, and if we let every little thing get to us, if we let people and events tear us down, it disrupts the peace of the 51FIFTY way of life.

The idea is to rise above the noise, the confusion, and the rest of the clutter so you can live your best life. Honestly, those core ideas help motivate me and inspire me to make positive things happen every day. That motivation is what keeps me on the right track (pun intended).

At heart, I'm a risk taker, and part of what I loved about the drug lifestyle was living on the edge. Racing has its own brand of excitement that brings those things together, but in a *healthful* way instead of an addictive one.

I get a surge of adrenaline from the speed of the car and the added benefit of feeding the part of myself that needs constant stimulation and new experiences. When I'm at the racetrack, I hear the fans cheering, and sometimes I sign autographs for them. They remind me of myself fifteen or twenty years ago—young adults looking for excitement, distraction, entertainment, and thrills. Back then, I found those things in the worst possible way, but now I see that if I can make such a big change, anyone can.

At the end of the day, when the race is over (no matter if I won or lost), instead of winding up passed out or in jail, I can go home to my family and my work with a satisfied mind, appreciating everything and everybody in my life with no feeling of wanting to escape.

I used and abused drugs for thirteen years, which turned me into a full-time, full-fledged addict. I tried to stop many times, but

I always went back to using. As you've read, it was a nightmare for me and those around me.

But since The Night—September 14, 2006—I have never looked back. I have never used cocaine. And those who stuck with me through it all will all agree on one thing . . . racing saved my life.

THE SCAR

This book is all about overcoming obstacles. When we are confronted with tough situations, we need to keep pushing forward.
Unfortunately, my personal struggles did not end when I stopped
using drugs. Years later, life once again hit me with another tough
challenge—the scar on my nose.

The scar, which you might be able to see in the photo on the
back of this book, has nothing to do with my drug use. In fact, at the
time the scar formed, in 2010, I was going through a wonderfully
positive and productive period. By that point, I'd been clean for
four years. I'd gotten my life back in order, regained the trust of my
friends and family, restored my self-confidence, and reconnected
with the person I was before I started using drugs.

The 51FIFTY brand was also growing, its profits fueling the
foundation. On the personal side, I had a great relationship with
Aysia and my daughters. I was also running and expanding the
family business.

But life had yet another curveball in store for me.

To understand what happened, we have to go back to 2003. That
was the year I decided to have an operation to correct my deviated
septum, which had caused breathing problems for me ever
since I was a kid. The surgery itself went great, but it left a slight
indentation on my nose. For years after the surgery, I would go to
the doctor, and he would give me a shot of a filler that decreased

the size of the indentation and made it less noticeable. It was a simple cosmetic procedure.

One day in 2010, I got the shot just as I had always done. But something went wrong, and the injection site became infected. Then the infection spread to my entire nose. It got so bad that I lost the skin on top of my nose, and in order for it to regrow, I had to have another operation. It never healed properly, and after battling the infection and suffering through skin reconstruction, I ended up with a very noticeable scar. And it wasn't going away.

I'd always been confident about my looks—that's part of who I am. In today's world, where looks are important and people can be judgmental, my scar became yet another obstacle I had to overcome. It was a huge setback to my sense of self-confidence.

At first, I felt self-conscious about it—a blemish so visible right in the middle of my face. I sometimes would look in the mirror and feel a huge sense of disappointment. Why did this happen to me? But I eventually realized that just as I had to move on from my addiction, I had to move on from worrying about that scar.

We all have scars of one kind or another. Much worse things happen to people every day than getting a scar on their nose. Self-acceptance is a huge part of growing up and getting through life. I soon realized that even though the scar had become part of me, I couldn't allow it to dictate who I am and what I could be.

I compare it to being a drug addict: I have scars from that experience, too, but those scars don't define me. They're a relic of who I was, but they don't have anything to do with who I am now. I've had to rise above what happened in the past to be able to live in the present. It's the same with the scar on my nose—I will not let it keep me from being the person I was always meant to be. I hope you won't let whatever tough situation you might be going through dictate your future, either. Believe in yourself and see yourself as the person you want to be. Then make it happen.

I'm glad to be alive, healthy, and committed to making this world a better place. It feels good to provide opportunities for the people around me. But most important, I'm happy that I can demonstrate my love for everyone in my life who stuck with me and never stopped believing in me. Because I know I didn't get here alone.

My wife, Aysia, played a huge part in my recovery. Without her, I would never have been able to make the positive changes I did and stay clean all these years. Our marriage has been a blessing. She is everything I could have ever asked for in a partner.

My parents were equally loving and supportive, and they did all they could for me, providing unconditional love. I know I put them through the wringer, but their love for me was always there.

Would I do it all again? No, I wouldn't. The broken marriages, the wasted hours and days, the years when my kids were growing up and I wasn't there, the lost time with loved ones—I want all that back again, but I can't have it. That missing time is like a scar: it will always be with me. I could have used those years to accomplish so much more both personally and professionally, but I was selfish, focused on all the wrong things.

One of the most important steps I want to take now is to thank everyone who played a part in helping me overcome my drug addiction and return to myself. Because of all the support I've received from family, friends, and the community, I'm able to give back. I'm able to use my past as a force for good and spend the rest of my life trying to make a positive mark on the world.

———————

Well, you've now read my story. You've seen the good and the evil. You know how I allowed myself to fall into the darkness of addiction and all its dangers. There was even the chance that I would never recover. With all the risks I was taking, I could have lost everything, including my life.

Experts in rehab tried to help me. But in the end, it was up to me to take hold of my destiny. I had to dig deep into my own psyche and find a new route to redemption. It had to be a permanent solution that would result in what I most wanted: to feel productive, to feel like myself, and to love others as I wanted them to love me.

To this day, I still have drug dreams, and sometimes I wake up holding my breath, as if I've just taken a hit. Other times I wake up feeling guilty for thinking that I'd done drugs the night before, even though it was only in a dream. Sometimes I even dream about getting caught or arrested again. The dreams are so vivid and realistic that it often takes a minute to reorient myself and remember that I have been clean for a long time now.

Today, I'm a lucky man to have found a pathway out of pain. Yes, it includes race car driving, hard work, and philanthropy, all positive outlets for my energy. But it wasn't easy getting to this point. I believe the devil sometimes touches us in mysterious ways—often by putting the wrong people around us. And while I feel strong today, I have to stay vigilant. God is with me. He has good plans for my life. He needs me. For reasons I might never understand, He wanted me to go down this path and find the redemption I did.

If you're struggling with anything in your own life—an addiction, a relationship problem, a financial challenge, a physical disease or disability—*know this*: there is always hope. There is always a solution. There is always a better approach to fueling your energy and healing yourself.

Knocking doors down was a key part of my process. We all have to knock them down from time to time in order to open a pathway to the future. I know from my own experience that it's hard to kick a new door open and walk through it.

But if I can do it, so can you. If I can help somebody else in pain, we all can.

The door is right in front of you. Whether you knock it down or just turn the key, there's a new life waiting on the other side of it.

RESOURCES

DRUGS 101

You might know someone in your life who is addicted to illegal or prescription drugs or alcohol. Or you might know someone who is addicted to overeating, gambling, or pornography. In fact, when it comes to cocaine addiction, there are, according to the Drug Enforcement Administration, 1.9 million coke users in the United States alone, and I was one of them.

No matter what the addiction, it's painful to see how it can completely derail the people around you. In an effort to understand a friend's or loved one's addiction, you might ask yourself, "Why is she not happy with her life?" The addict might have a great job, a supportive spouse, healthy kids, and plenty of money. You might wonder, "What more does she need?" But it's not about need. It's about the emotional forces that drive a person to seek an escape from pain, from pressure, from worry.

Temptations are all around us. You will drive yourself crazy trying to figure out what other people need, even if they're close to you and you know them well. It could be your wife, your brother, or your teenage son, but you won't be able to influence that person's choices. Your love won't heal addicted people. They have to heal themselves.

Unless you are an addict yourself or trained as an addiction counselor, you won't understand why someone would keep using drugs, despite all the trouble and pain it causes, even when that person seems to have a good life that "should" be enough to keep him clean.

For me, the attraction of drugs and the lifestyle that went along with them were more appealing than you can imagine. Yes, despite all the inherent risks and dangers of what I did, it was still irresistible to me at the time. Most people only see the bad side of drug use as depicted on TV and in movies, but there is an entirely different perspective when you're the person who is addicted.

The drug lifestyle offers complete freedom. You have no obligations, no responsibilities, nothing to answer for, and no one to answer to. There are no time constraints and no structures to follow. You don't have to take care of anybody (including yourself). Your only obligation is to make sure your supply doesn't run out. You have to stay high. You have to plan for it, which is why I would typically call my dealer even when my stash was still half full.

Another part of the appeal is that you're not part of the regular world. You break out of the norm, become a rebel, and that's exciting, too. While the rest of the world is sleeping or going through the drudgery of work, you're out roaming around, looking for trouble. I remember intentionally looking for cops to outrun and risks to take. Anything to get my blood going.

You also have a sense of belonging to the party culture. Your fellow drug users become your tribe, your community. It's the same reason people are attracted to gangs. It gives you someplace to belong, a social system full of brothers and sisters who care about the same things you care about.

In the drug world, no user can ever know what will be the one thing that finally kills him. Most addicts are in denial of all the risks, including death, and are consumed with getting high at any cost. With all the substances available today, the first time you try a drug could be your last. I'm not preaching, but no user is stronger than an addictive drug. *No one is.*

When I started out, I had no idea how much power cocaine had over me or how far down I could fall. But I now know that the only way to avoid that descent is to stay away from drugs in the first place. I felt like I was completely in control of my drug use and my life, but cocaine taught me that I wasn't in control at all. I was lying to myself. I was in denial. Even today, after years of being clean, I know that if I start playing around with cocaine again, if I let it into my life, it would take over completely. I'd be right back where I used to be, and the beautiful life I've built for myself would end.

Drugs don't care who you are or where you come from or how much money you have or how you were raised. They will take over any life and destroy it. Even if you think, as I did, that you are totally in control of everything in your life, when you find that one drug that hits the spot for you, it will grab hold of you like nothing you can ever imagine. It stops *everything*: it stops your life, it stops your personal growth and cognitive development, and it stops *time*.

One of the big things I learned in rehab is about the loss of time—the years you spend disconnected from relationships and human life and the price you pay for that disconnection.

What does this mean? It means that when you're doing drugs, you are kind of caught in a time bubble, where things stay pretty much the same while the rest of the world moves on. Some say it takes one year to catch up for every year you lost. In my case, it's taken me ten years to catch up, to mentally and spiritually connect with the normal world.

After you get clean, you expect everything and everyone to still be where you left them ten years earlier. But it's a big shock when you discover that they're *not* the same, because they've moved on.

They've grown and evolved, as healthy people should, and now you're ten years behind them.

The time bubble also causes problems with forgiveness, because people need time to heal from the pain you've caused them. Once you get clean, you have years of damage control to address. You were lost in time, and while you were gone, your loved ones suffered and struggled every day. Now that you're clean and you feel better, you expect them to feel better, too. But forgiveness is a long process. It's not instant.

The good news is that no matter how far gone someone is, change *is* possible. Lots of drug users believe that addicts can never change and will remain stuck in an endless loop of bingeing, getting clean, and bingeing again, forever. When I was using, my drug friends told me that being drug-free was not the real me and I should accept the fact that I would be an addict for life. I would tell them that my binge was only temporary and that I could figure a way out of that lifestyle.

But the other addicts would laugh and say, "Yeah, right. Once an addict, always an addict!" I think they told me these things because that's how they felt about themselves. I also think they wanted company in their addiction: they needed the sense of brotherhood and community that comes with the lifestyle.

The reason I was a binge user instead of a daily user was because I really wanted to do well at my job, and I couldn't function normally at work if I was high. There were too many critical decisions to make every single day, and I couldn't do that while on drugs. I opted to do all my drugs at once, during long binge periods when I'd stay high for weeks until either my body shut down or I got arrested. Then I'd go to rehab, get clean, and go back to work . . . until my next binge.

There *are* people who can function in their daily lives while under the influence. They're called functioning addicts or alcoholics, and there are millions of them. They manage to appear normal and sober, and in some cases, they're quite successful in their high-powered careers, all while consuming alcohol or drugs. But that wasn't me at all. I tried but failed at functioning while high.

One thing I learned from all the mistakes I made is how to be more forgiving of others. I did some terrible things, yet people forgave me because they loved me. So that meant I had to forgive myself, too. I also learned how to let go of my judgments about others, especially other addicts who've had it rough and behave unscrupulously because they're emotionally damaged.

I get it. Maybe their addictions were triggered by their upbringing, some abuse or neglect or trauma that caused incredible pain. Even though drug use isn't the solution, I can understand the desire to numb the pain. There is so much family dysfunction in the world, which is why I never forget how blessed I am to have been raised in such a supportive and loving family. My mother and father were fantastic parents who gave us the kind of values and love that all children deserve.

Yet I still was susceptible to drug addiction. It was as if evil itself took me over. I believe there really is an evil force known as the devil, and for addicts, it takes control. At the same time, you have to hope that the opposite force—God—is trying to save you each and every minute. There were times when I was scared shitless as I followed the path the devil was taking me on. But I believed God was watching over me. He knew that I was a good person and wouldn't hurt anyone. It was a constant struggle, and that's the state in which I lived for thirteen years of active addiction.

I intend to stay clean for the rest of my life. But in order to do that, there are some essential things I need to do. These techniques worked for me, and I hope they can work for others as well.

1. **STAY AWAY FROM PEOPLE WHO DO DRUGS.** This means you need to step away from toxic friends, even those who might be close to you. It can also mean changing your relationship with your spouse or partner, through separation or even divorce.

2. **STAY AWAY FROM PLACES** where drugs are normally found or used.

3. **FIND POSITIVE HABITS** to replace negative patterns. For example, stop smoking cigarettes or overeating and start exercising.

4. **MAKE CHANGES TO YOUR DAILY ROUTINE.** It's important to change things you've been doing while you were on drugs, because old habits and routines can easily keep you locked into the aspects of your former life. So change it up. Add something new, like taking a walk every morning. Find a new hobby. Hang out at a new coffee place.

5. **IMPROVE YOUR DIET.** Limit junk food, fast food, and processed food. Eat more fruits and vegetables. Learn to cook/food prep if you don't already know how. Eat meals at regularly scheduled times.

6. **ELIMINATE TRIGGERS.** Stay away from people, places, and things that remind you of your old behaviors. Hold yourself accountable and realize your drug addiction is stronger than your willpower.

7. **DON'T GET OVERWHELMED** by the massive task of getting clean and staying clean forever. As the saying goes, take it *one day at a time*. Do the right thing now, in this moment, then again in the next moment, and so on. You feel a sense of achievement, and the momentum builds, which is why staying clean and sober gets easier over time.

8. **STAY BUSY.** As I've said several times, being bored is a huge trigger for using drugs. Organize your time. Plan your activities. You have to be engaged in life, doing something positive. It can be reading, solving puzzles, traveling, learning a new sport, or volunteering—virtually anything that affects you in a positive way.

9. **GET OUT OF THE HOUSE.** Reach out to good friends for socializing. Stay connected. Be part of the world in a positive way. Isolation is the breeding ground for addiction, and I spent too many years alone, hiding from the world.

No matter what you do, no matter how long you stay clean, there will always be new challenges, some of which you could never have anticipated. There are times when I feel especially stressed by my business or my family and my peace of mind is disturbed. When that happens, I will stop and pray to God and thank God for the strength that He has given me to push away the devil. If you follow the guidelines, you, too, will become stronger and more able to deal with stressful situations and less likely to resort to drug use or any other addiction you have.

DRUGS IN EVERYDAY LIFE

What are mind-altering substances? Do alcohol and cigarettes qualify as drugs?

Most drug rehab facilities tell you that alcohol is a drug, classified as a central nervous system depressant. Yes, in small quantities, it can feel great to drink and loosen up. But drinkers need to know that alcohol is a disinhibitor that slows down brain functioning, resulting in slurred speech, unsteady movement, disturbed perceptions, and an inability to react quickly.

So yes, alcohol is a powerful drug. If you do your research, you will find out that nicotine is a drug as well, and a very addictive one. To be completely clean of all drugs, a person needs to be a nonsmoker and alcohol-free.

But what about caffeine? Most of us enjoy the caffeine in coffee, tea, and energy drinks. Does that make us all addicts? How far do we go when it comes to calling substances addictive?

This is where I think we all need to think for ourselves about what's reasonable and moderate, what's best for our health, and what's best for allowing us to live the life we want to. For example,

I was never a big drinker, so I never abused alcohol. I'm not saying I haven't gotten drunk at times over the years, but alcohol never got hold of me like cocaine did, causing me to binge day after day. I never missed work because of it, and it did not disrupt my family life.

So why did I choose to stop drinking for that one year when I first decided to get clean? Because I wanted to be free from *all* mind-altering substances so my self-control wouldn't be compromised.

When it came to cigarettes, this addiction wasn't easy to kick. I started smoking in college and continued to smoke for many years. Knowing the health risks, I would stop and start all the time, but I never quit for longer than a few months. I would eventually end up bumming a cigarette when I was drinking with friends, and that pattern would repeat itself again and again, until finally I bought my own pack.

What made me want to quit smoking cigarettes forever? I knew deep down I wasn't a smoker. I wanted to be healthy. I knew smoking was a disgusting habit that affected how I looked, smelled, and even behaved. It kept me from exercising and eating properly. It was also a big confidence killer, especially as people came to understand more about the harmful effects of secondhand smoke.

I also hated having to step outside once the state government made smoking against the law in buildings throughout California. It felt like I was being controlled by another substance, which in fact I was. When you're a smoker, you're always thinking about where you're going and whom you'll be with so you'll be sure you can have a cigarette when you need one. Once you stop, it frees you to never think about that again. Quitting was one of the most important factors in helping me be a better person, mentally and physically.

As I said, there are many different types of rehab—some free, some quite expensive. What worked for me might not be what works best for other addicts. That's okay. Whatever it takes. No addict needs to feel as if he or she can't recover because rehab is financially unaffordable. Some insurance programs cover the cost of rehab. But even if you have to pay, there are a variety of options with various costs associated with each.

For daily support, twelve-step programs such as Alcoholics Anonymous and Narcotics Anonymous are available in most cities and are, of course, absolutely free and quite popular. These programs are especially helpful for recovering addicts who may not have emotional support from family or friends. Recovery meetings are a great place to talk with others about your experience.

But no matter what form of treatment you choose, it only works when you're truly ready to stop. You have to find the willingness to give it your all each and every time you have a relapse and enter rehab. And that isn't easy.

TRIGGERS

Have you ever started a new diet, but something triggers you to start eating the same old foods again? You swore off potato chips, pretzels, cupcakes, and cookies, right? Your willpower and discipline work beautifully—until you go to a birthday party. There's a delicious-looking chocolate cake sitting there, and it would be rude to refuse a piece, right? Some people at the party may even pressure you, saying, "One little piece won't hurt."

The party, the pressure, the polite suggestions, and the cake are all *triggers*, which means that something, someone, or simply an idea or a familiar feeling can kick-start the urge to indulge.

It's the same thing with drugs. So often, people want to stop using drugs, but they don't want to change their lifestyle. In other words, they want to keep the same friends and go to the same places, essentially lying to themselves about how strong they are. If you're serious about giving up fattening foods, for example, you can't go to a birthday party or bakery and expect yourself to "just say no." To put it another way, if you go into a barbershop, you're going to get a haircut.

Following are some of my past triggers.

1. **BOREDOM** is my biggest challenge—a feeling of total disinterest, as if there's nothing to do and life is dull. I still struggle with this when I have days off. Even though I don't use drugs anymore, when I get bored, I am really off my game.

2. **A FIGHT WITH A FAMILY MEMBER.** If you look at the patterns in my behavior, you can see that I sometimes went on huge binges in response to major conflicts with my wives or family members, and those binges always ended badly.

3. **STRESS** is one of the most common triggers for addicts. Problems or pressures in your life start piling up, and you feel anxious, depressed, nervous, or overwhelmed. You think just one hit will "take the edge off." But that kind of thinking is dangerous for an addict, because there's never just *one* hit. The first one kicks off a binge.

4. **ALCOHOL.** Everyone knows your inhibitions are down when you are drinking, and too much alcohol can make drugs seem appealing and affect your ability to resist them.

5. **EUPHORIC RECALL.** Thinking about the good times when you were high, remembering how it felt, can be a powerful trigger. I felt awesome when I was using, but as an addict, if you dwell on that feeling, it can trigger your desire to use again.

6. **ESCAPE FANTASY.** Who doesn't want to be free of responsibility? Binges were *fun*. Wanting to escape from reality can be a huge temptation, very hard to resist.

7. **APPETITE FOR EXCITEMENT.** The risk and excitement in the drug lifestyle has a very strong appeal for some people. In my case, it was the one and only thing that alleviated my boredom.

8. **EXPOSURE TO DRUG-ASSOCIATED PEOPLE, PLACES, AND THINGS.** Certain friends, like those who insist you eat cake, can tempt you to use drugs. Wanting to be accepted, to have fun, and to be part of the crowd are reasons why you might want to spend time with your drug buddies or hang out in places where drugs are available. But you've got to detach yourself from those people. It's nothing personal. Being around them is not healthy.

9. **SEXUAL FANTASY.** The sensation of having sex on drugs can be a strong hook. Your inhibitions are down; you do things you might not ordinarily want to do. It might be incredibly exciting at the time, but it can lead to having regrets. While I won't go into graphic detail here, sex on drugs is obviously different from sex that's connected to loving emotion and caring.

BOTTOM LINE: No two people are alike, and we all need to figure out who we are, how we're triggered, and what changes we need to make in our lives. While I certainly can't tell you how to change your life, I can share with you what has helped me, the lessons I've learned through all the ups and downs of my life experience.

To keep myself straight, I use all the tools I've learned on a daily basis. This gives me the strength and focus to take care of my family, my wife and children, my job, my foundation, and everything else I care about.

I also pray daily, thanking God for every blessing. Because even after all these years of being clean, I'm still aware that evil is around me, trying to take me back to drugs. I have to look to God to keep me straight. I have to have faith that I can do it one day at a time. The struggle is still there inside me, and honestly, I live with that truth. Now, every time I'm feeling tired or stressed, or when I have an important decision to make, I ask myself, *What would a 51FIFTY person do?* You know the answer.

ACKNOWLEDGMENTS

I want to start by thanking my wife, Aysia, for helping me transform my life. I met her in 2006, at the end of my darkest days, and she is now beside me during the brightest ones.

I also want to thank my two beautiful daughters, Elaina and Morgan, for giving me strength each and every day. I know that during their early years, I often failed at being an attentive father. (And I failed at being a husband to my two previous wives.) All I can do now is be there for my daughters, show them my love, and let them know how much they mean to me. I am proud of who they have become, and I hope they can forgive me for my mistakes.

To my parents, what can I say? I put them through hell, yet they still stood by me. I have deep regrets about how much suffering I caused them because of my personal challenges. They provided me and my siblings with a good home, endless love, and every opportunity to create a positive, fulfilling life. I would not have made it this far without their enduring support.

I have also been blessed with some of the best friends anyone could ask for, many of them dating back to early childhood. They were always there to help when I needed it, and for that, I will be eternally grateful.

When I think about the heartbreak I caused, I regret it all. I know I can't get that time back. All I can do is share the best parts of myself and the constructive, healthy life that has given me a sense of inner peace. I'm spending it with the people I love. I can only thank them for keeping me in their hearts all these years. I could have not done it without them. Because of the support I've received, I am able to give back by turning my troubled past into a story that can, with any luck, provide hope, help, and healing to others.

Thank you.

ABOUT THE AUTHOR

American businessman and philanthropist Carlos Vieira is the vice president of A. V. Thomas Produce, the largest producer of organic and conventional sweet potatoes in the United States, established by his great-uncle in 1960. He is also the founder of the Carlos Vieira Foundation, which sponsors three initiatives—the Race for Autism, the Race 2B Drug Free, and the Race to End the Stigma—dedicated to raising awareness of autism, addiction, and mental illness. Vieira, born in 1972, is also a competitive race car driver and the owner of the number 51 car, competing in various race series throughout the West Coast. He is the creator and CEO of the lifestyle brand 51FIFTY, which is about believing in yourself, exploring who you are, and discovering who you want to be in order to live life to its fullest. Vieira is the recipient of the Portuguese Education Foundation Businessman of the Year Award and the Portuguese Fraternal Society of America Portuguese Community Service Award. The father of two daughters, Vieira lives with his wife, Aysia, in Atwater, California.

CONTACT:

✉ carlos@carlosvieirafoundation.org
🅕 facebook.com/CarlosEVieira